BITCOIN
AND MARKET TALES

Unmasking the Crypto Manipulators

All Rights Reserved
Copyright © 2024

By

Michael Eddleman

First Edition

July 21, 2024

Disclaimer

The information contained in this book, *Bitcoin Whales and Market Tales - Unmasking the Crypto Manipulators* (the "Book"), is provided for educational and informational purposes only. The author, Michael Eddleman, and the publisher make no representations or warranties of any kind, express or implied, about the completeness, accuracy, reliability, suitability, or availability of the information, products, services, or related graphics contained in this Book for any purpose. Any reliance you place on such information is therefore strictly at your own risk.

No Legal, Financial, or Investment Advice

The content of this Book is not intended to be a substitute for professional legal, financial, or investment advice. The author and the publisher are not licensed financial advisors, attorneys, or accountants. Readers should seek the advice of qualified professionals regarding any legal, financial, or investment decisions. The strategies, analysis, and opinions expressed in this Book are the author's own and do not constitute legal, financial, or investment advice.

No Endorsement of Illegal Activities

This Book contains discussions of market behaviors, including but not limited to, market manipulation tactics such as pump-and-dump schemes and wash trading. The inclusion of such discussions is solely for the purpose of illustrating market phenomena and does not constitute endorsement, encouragement, or promotion of illegal activities. The author and publisher expressly disavow any intent to assist, advise, or encourage any person in any way to engage in any unlawful activity or to violate any laws or regulations.

No Warranties and Limitation of Liability

The author and publisher make no warranties, either express or implied, regarding the legality of the content in this Book or the legality of actions taken based on the information contained herein. The author and publisher will not be held liable for any damages or losses of any kind arising out of the use of or reliance on this Book or any content contained within it, including but not limited to indirect, incidental, punitive, and consequential damages.

Personal Opinions

The views and opinions expressed in this Book are those of the author and do not necessarily reflect the official policy or position of any other individual, agency, organization, employer, or company. The author's opinions are based on personal research and understanding and should not be interpreted as factual statements.

No Guarantees of Outcomes

The Book provides insights into market behaviors and strategies, but it does not guarantee any specific outcomes. The cryptocurrency markets are highly volatile and subject to a wide range of influences beyond the control of the author or publisher. Readers are urged to conduct their own independent research and consult with professionals before making any decisions based on the information provided in this Book.

Jurisdiction and Compliance

This Book is intended to be compliant with the laws and regulations of the United States. The author and publisher do not guarantee compliance with the laws of any other jurisdiction. Readers are responsible for ensuring that their actions comply with local laws and regulations.

Reserved Rights

The author and publisher reserve the right to amend or update the content of this Book and its associated disclaimers at any time without prior notice.

Foreword by the Author

In the dawn of the digital age, Bitcoin emerged as a beacon of innovation, promising a decentralized and transparent financial revolution. It captivated the imaginations of visionaries, technologists, and investors, heralding a new era where financial systems were free from the constraints of traditional intermediaries. Bitcoin's immutable blockchain technology and finite supply of 21 million coins were designed to offer stability and trust in a world often plagued by economic uncertainties and centralized control.

However, as with all revolutionary ideas, Bitcoin's journey has been anything but linear. Its path has been marked by unprecedented volatility, speculative fervor, and, most intriguingly, the hidden machinations of powerful market players—whales who possess the ability to manipulate and sway the market to their advantage. This book delves deep into the enigmatic world of Bitcoin, uncovering the truth behind its unpredictable price movements and the covert strategies employed by these crypto manipulators.

"Bitcoin Whales and Market Tales" is not just a chronicle of market behavior; it is a wake-up call to the crypto community and beyond. Through meticulous research and analysis, this book exposes the sophisticated tactics of market manipulators and illuminates the broader implications for the future of Bitcoin and the cryptocurrency market as a whole. It challenges the prevailing narratives of natural market dynamics and invites readers to question the forces that shape the financial landscape of digital currencies.

As the author, my journey into the world of Bitcoin has been one of relentless curiosity and a quest for truth. The complexities of Bitcoin's market behavior, the contradictions within its design, and the powerful influence of its largest holders have all compelled me to share these insights with you. This book is a culmination of that endeavor—a comprehensive exploration aimed at educating and empowering traders, investors, and anyone intrigued by the world of cryptocurrencies.

In these pages, you will find a detailed examination of the tools and strategies used by whales to orchestrate massive price movements, insights into the regulatory challenges and potential solutions for creating a more transparent and stable market environment, and practical advice for recognizing and navigating the signs of manipulation. Whether you are a seasoned trader, a new investor, or simply curious about the intricacies of the Bitcoin market, this book offers invaluable knowledge and guidance.

Ultimately, "Bitcoin Whales and Market Tales" is a call to action. It urges the Bitcoin community to strive for greater transparency and fairness, to recognize the signs of manipulation, and to advocate for regulatory measures that protect the integrity of the market. By doing so, we can work towards realizing Bitcoin's original promise of a decentralized, fair, and sustainable financial system.

I invite you to join me on this journey of discovery and enlightenment. Let us uncover the hidden forces at play, understand the true nature of Bitcoin's market dynamics, and together, pave the way for a future where digital currencies can thrive in an environment of trust and transparency.

Michael Eddleman
July 2024

TABLE OF CONTENTS

PREFACE 10

   INTRODUCTION TO BITCOIN'S PARADOX 10
   THE PURPOSE OF THIS BOOK 12
   ACKNOWLEDGEMENTS 14

PROLOGUE 17

   THE PROMISE OF BITCOIN 17
   EARLY OPTIMISM VS. MARKET REALITY 19
   A CALL FOR INVESTIGATION 21

CHAPTER 1: UNDERSTANDING BITCOIN'S DESIGN AND STRUCTURE 24

   THE FUNDAMENTALS OF BITCOIN 24
      What is Bitcoin? 24
      The Blockchain Technology 26
      The 21 Million Cap 28
   THE MARKET DYNAMICS OF BITCOIN 30
      Supply and Demand Basics 30
      Bitcoin as Digital Gold 32
      Market Participants 35
   CHALLENGES IN BITCOIN VALUATION 37
      Price Discovery Mechanisms 37
      Volatility Factors 40
      Real vs. Perceived Value 42

CHAPTER 2: THE MYTH OF NATURAL FLUCTUATIONS 46

   ANALYZING VOLATILITY 46
      Historical Price Movements 46
      Common Explanations 48
      Inadequacies of Traditional Explanations 50
   MANIPULATION TECHNIQUES 53
      Pump and Dump Schemes 53
      Wash Trading 55
      Coordinated Market Manipulation 57
   IMPACT OF SPECULATION 60

    Role of Speculators *60*
    Behavioral Economics *62*
    Market Psychology *64*

CHAPTER 3: THE WHALES: WHO THEY ARE AND WHAT THEY DO 68

  IDENTIFYING THE WHALES 68
    Definition of a Whale *68*
    Whale Strategies *70*
    Whales vs. Retail Investors *72*
  WHALE ACTIVITIES AND MARKET IMPACT 74
    Case Studies of Whale Movements *74*
    Large Transactions and Price Swings *76*
    The Ripple Effect *79*
  THE ETHICS AND LEGALITY OF WHALE BEHAVIOR 81
    Ethical Considerations *81*
    Legal Framework *84*
    Mitigating Manipulation *87*

CHAPTER 4: THE TOOLS OF MANIPULATION 90

  TECHNICAL ANALYSIS AND ITS MISUSE 90
    Basics of Technical Analysis *90*
    Manipulative Tactics Using Technical Analysis *92*
    Impact on Trader Behavior *94*
  MEDIA AND INFORMATION CONTROL 97
    Role of Media in Bitcoin Market *97*
    Misinformation and Its Effects *100*
    Counteracting Misinformation *102*
  DARK POOLS AND OFF-EXCHANGE TRADING 105
    Understanding Dark Pools *105*
    Off-Exchange Trading Mechanisms *107*
    Implications for Market Integrity *109*

CHAPTER 5: REGULATORY PERSPECTIVES AND CHALLENGES 113

  CURRENT REGULATORY LANDSCAPE 113
    Global Regulatory Environment *113*
    Major Regulatory Bodies *116*

    Recent Regulatory Developments *118*
  CHALLENGES IN REGULATING BITCOIN 121
    Decentralization vs. Regulation *121*
    Anonymity and Privacy Issues *124*
    Jurisdictional Conflicts *127*
  FUTURE OF BITCOIN REGULATION 130
    Potential Regulatory Models *130*
    Impact of Regulation on Market *133*
    Roadmap for Effective Regulation *136*

CHAPTER 6: THE FUTURE OF BITCOIN 140

  SCENARIOS FOR BITCOIN'S FUTURE 140
    Bullish Scenarios *140*
    Bearish Scenarios *142*
    Realistic Projections *145*
  INNOVATIONS AND TECHNOLOGICAL ADVANCES 147
    Layer 2 Solutions *147*
    Integrating with Traditional Finance *149*
    Emerging Technologies *151*
  BITCOIN IN THE GLOBAL ECONOMY 153
    Bitcoin as Legal Tender *153*
    Bitcoin's Role in Financial Inclusion *155*
    Bitcoin and Geopolitics *157*

CHAPTER 7: PROTECTING YOURSELF IN THE BITCOIN MARKET 160

  RISK MANAGEMENT STRATEGIES 160
    Diversification *160*
    Stop Loss and Take Profit *162*
    Staying Informed *164*
  RECOGNIZING MANIPULATIVE PATTERNS 167
    Identifying Red Flags *167*
    Analyzing Market Sentiment *169*
    Protecting Against FOMO and FUD *170*
  BEST PRACTICES FOR TRADING AND INVESTING 172
    Long-term vs. Short-term Strategies *172*

Leveraging Technology..174
Continuous Learning and Adaptation..........................176
CONCLUSION..179
SUMMARIZING KEY INSIGHTS..179
THE PATH FORWARD FOR BITCOIN 180
FINAL THOUGHTS ON MARKET INTEGRITY AND STABILITY 182

Preface

Introduction to Bitcoin's Paradox

Bitcoin, the pioneering cryptocurrency, was introduced with the promise of revolutionizing the financial system. Its design as a decentralized and transparent form of digital currency seemed to offer a secure and stable alternative to traditional financial systems. Bitcoin's decentralized nature, underpinned by blockchain technology, and its finite supply cap of 21 million units suggested that it would function as a stable and appreciating asset. However, the reality of Bitcoin's market behavior starkly contrasts with these expectations. Instead of stability, Bitcoin is notorious for its extreme volatility, with prices swinging wildly within short periods. This paradox raises critical questions about the factors driving such fluctuations and the integrity of the market itself.

At its core, Bitcoin was envisioned as a response to the flaws of centralized financial systems. Its blockchain technology ensures that every transaction is recorded on a public ledger, accessible to anyone and immutable once confirmed. This transparency and security were intended to eliminate the need for intermediaries, reduce transaction costs, and provide a democratized financial ecosystem. The fixed supply cap of 21 million Bitcoins was designed to protect against inflation, a common issue with fiat currencies that can be printed at will by central banks. In theory, these attributes should create a stable and appreciating value as demand for Bitcoin increases.

However, Bitcoin's market behavior reveals a different story. The price of Bitcoin has been subject to extreme volatility, influenced by speculation and market manipulation. The significant price fluctuations are often attributed to the activities of large holders, known as "whales," who can influence the market with their substantial holdings. These whales, by owning a large portion of the Bitcoin supply, have the power to manipulate prices through coordinated buying and selling, creating artificial highs and lows to maximize their profits. This manipulation distorts the natural supply and demand dynamics, leading to unpredictable market movements that can result in significant losses for unsuspecting traders.

The tools and strategies employed by these manipulators are sophisticated and multifaceted. Techniques such as wash trading, where an investor simultaneously buys and sells the same financial instruments to create misleading market activity, and pump and dump schemes, where the price of an asset is artificially inflated to attract investors before being sold off at a profit, are commonly used. These tactics create an illusion of market sentiment, driving irrational behavior among traders and exacerbating volatility. The impact of such manipulation is profound, undermining the foundational principles of Bitcoin and raising questions about its sustainability as a store of value.

The broader implications of this market manipulation extend beyond individual losses. They challenge the very essence of Bitcoin's promise as a decentralized and fair financial system. The concentration of power in the hands of a few large players contradicts the ideals of decentralization and democratization that Bitcoin was supposed to represent. This centralization of influence can erode trust in the cryptocurrency market, deterring new investors and stifling innovation. Furthermore, it highlights the urgent need for regulatory measures to address these manipulative practices and foster a more transparent and stable market environment.

While Bitcoin's volatility and susceptibility to manipulation present significant challenges, they also offer valuable lessons for traders and investors. Recognizing the signs of market manipulation and understanding the underlying dynamics can help market participants make more informed decisions. By staying vigilant and employing risk management strategies, traders can navigate the complexities of the Bitcoin market and mitigate potential losses. Moreover, the push for regulatory oversight and greater transparency can contribute to a healthier and more sustainable cryptocurrency ecosystem.

Bitcoin's paradox of being a revolutionary yet volatile asset underscores the complexities of its market dynamics. The interplay between its decentralized design and the manipulative practices of powerful market players creates a challenging environment for investors. As the cryptocurrency market continues to evolve, addressing these issues is crucial for realizing Bitcoin's original promise and ensuring its role in the future of finance.

The Purpose of this Book

In a world where digital currencies are increasingly capturing the public's imagination and investment dollars, understanding the nuances of Bitcoin is crucial. This book is crafted to unravel the intricate web of Bitcoin's market behavior and shed light on the forces that drive its volatility. At its essence, the purpose of this book is to provide readers with a comprehensive understanding of Bitcoin's unique position in the financial landscape, its inherent contradictions, and the mechanisms behind its unpredictable price movements.

Bitcoin was introduced as a revolutionary alternative to traditional financial systems, promising decentralization, transparency, and a fixed supply cap that ostensibly protected against inflation. Its emergence was heralded as the dawn of a new era in finance, where control over money would no longer be concentrated in the hands of a few but distributed across a network of users. This utopian vision was underpinned by blockchain technology, which promised secure and transparent transactions. However, the reality has often diverged from this ideal.

The primary aim of this book is to dissect the paradox of Bitcoin's volatility in the face of its purported stability. Despite its decentralized structure and finite supply, Bitcoin's market is characterized by extreme price fluctuations. These swings are not merely the result of natural market dynamics but are significantly influenced by deliberate actions of powerful market participants. The book delves into the roles of these key players, often referred to as 'whales,' who possess the ability to sway the market in their favor due to their substantial Bitcoin holdings.

By illuminating the strategies and tactics employed by these manipulators, such as coordinated buying and selling, wash trading, and pump-and-dump schemes, this book aims to educate readers on recognizing the signs of market manipulation. Understanding these manipulative practices is essential for anyone looking to invest in or trade Bitcoin, as it enables them to make more informed decisions and avoid falling prey to market machinations.

Furthermore, the book explores the broader implications of Bitcoin's market behavior for its future as a viable financial asset. It raises critical questions about Bitcoin's sustainability as a store of value and its potential to fulfill its original promise of a decentralized and fair financial system. The discussion extends to the potential regulatory measures that could mitigate these manipulative practices and foster a more transparent and stable market environment. By examining these issues, the book provides a roadmap for creating a healthier cryptocurrency ecosystem.

In addition to offering insights into the manipulation and volatility of the Bitcoin market, the book also aims to empower readers by providing practical advice on risk management and trading strategies. It emphasizes the importance of vigilance, continuous learning, and adaptability in navigating the complexities of the Bitcoin market. By staying informed and employing sound trading practices, investors can better protect themselves against the inherent risks of this volatile asset.

Ultimately, this book serves as a wake-up call to the Bitcoin community and beyond. It challenges prevailing narratives about Bitcoin's price volatility and exposes the hidden forces at play. Whether you are a seasoned trader, a new investor, or simply curious about the world of cryptocurrencies, this book offers invaluable insights into the complexities of the Bitcoin market and the urgent need for greater transparency and fairness. Through meticulous research and analysis, it seeks to foster a deeper understanding of Bitcoin's true nature and guide readers toward a more informed and strategic approach to engaging with this groundbreaking digital currency.

Acknowledgements

Creating this book has been a collaborative endeavor, and it is important to acknowledge the many contributions that have made it possible. I am deeply grateful to my family for their unwavering support and patience. Their encouragement has been a constant source of motivation throughout this project.

I extend my sincere thanks to the numerous experts and professionals who generously shared their insights and knowledge on Bitcoin and the broader cryptocurrency market. Their expertise has been invaluable in providing a comprehensive understanding of the subject matter. Special appreciation goes to those who participated in interviews, offered data, and provided critical feedback, enriching the content and ensuring its accuracy.

My gratitude goes to my colleagues, whose intellectual contributions and critical discussions have greatly influenced the direction of this book. Their dedication to exploring the complexities of Bitcoin has been instrumental in shaping the final product. I am particularly thankful for the collaborative spirit and commitment to excellence that my colleagues have demonstrated.

I would also like to acknowledge the editorial team for their meticulous attention to detail and dedication to ensuring the book's clarity and coherence. Their hard work in refining the manuscript has been essential in transforming the initial drafts into a polished and professional final product.

Furthermore, I am thankful to the various institutions and organizations that provided the necessary resources and platforms for my research. Access to libraries, online databases, and industry conferences has been indispensable in gathering the information required for this book.

To the Bitcoin and cryptocurrency community, I express my gratitude for your passion and innovation. The vibrant discussions, debates, and shared knowledge within this community have significantly informed my understanding and perspective on the subject. Your collective contributions have played a pivotal role in shaping the discourse on Bitcoin and its impact on the financial world.

I would like to extend my appreciation to the reviewers and beta readers who provided invaluable feedback on early versions of this manuscript. Their constructive criticism and insightful suggestions have been instrumental in enhancing the clarity and coherence of the arguments presented.

Lastly, I thank my publisher for believing in this project and providing the support needed to bring it to a global audience. Their professionalism and dedication to promoting important discussions about the future of finance are truly commendable.

This book is the result of a collective effort, and I am deeply appreciative of everyone who has contributed to its creation. Thank you for your support, guidance, and belief in the importance of exploring the intricacies of Bitcoin and its impact on the financial system.

Prologue

The Promise of Bitcoin

Bitcoin emerged with the promise of revolutionizing the financial system by introducing a decentralized, transparent, and secure form of digital currency. Its creation was driven by a vision to eliminate the control of traditional financial institutions and provide an alternative that could be trusted by people around the world. The underlying technology, blockchain, ensured that every transaction was recorded on a public ledger, making it virtually tamper-proof and immune to fraud. This revolutionary approach aimed to democratize finance, reduce transaction costs, and offer a hedge against inflation through its fixed supply cap of 21 million Bitcoins.

The initial promise of Bitcoin was rooted in its potential to address several flaws in the traditional financial system. Central banks and financial institutions have long been criticized for their lack of transparency, high transaction fees, and the ability to manipulate the money supply. Bitcoin, by design, was intended to be free from these issues. The fixed supply of Bitcoin was seen as a safeguard against the arbitrary expansion of money supply, which often leads to inflation and devaluation of currency in traditional systems.

Bitcoin's decentralized nature was another cornerstone of its promise. Unlike traditional currencies that are controlled by central banks, Bitcoin operates on a peer-to-peer network. This means that no single entity has control over the entire system. Transactions are verified by network participants known as miners, who use their computing power to solve complex mathematical problems. This process, known as mining, not only secures the network but also introduces new Bitcoins into circulation in a controlled manner.

Transparency is another key aspect of Bitcoin's promise. All transactions are recorded on the blockchain, a public ledger that is accessible to anyone. This level of transparency ensures that transactions can be independently verified, reducing the risk of fraud and corruption. It also means that the history of each Bitcoin can be traced back to its origin, providing a level of accountability that is absent in traditional financial systems.

The fixed supply cap of 21 million Bitcoins is designed to counteract the inflationary pressures that plague fiat currencies. In traditional financial systems, central banks can print money at will, leading to inflation and reducing the purchasing power of the currency. Bitcoin's fixed supply ensures that it remains scarce, and as demand for it increases, its value is expected to rise. This deflationary characteristic has led to Bitcoin being compared to digital gold, a store of value that can protect against the erosion of wealth.

However, the journey of Bitcoin has not been without challenges. Despite its promise of stability and security, Bitcoin has been subject to extreme volatility. Its price has experienced dramatic swings, often driven by speculation and market manipulation. The activities of large holders, known as whales, who control significant portions of the Bitcoin supply, have led to concerns about market manipulation. These whales have the power to influence prices through coordinated buying and selling, creating artificial highs and lows to maximize their profits.

Despite these challenges, the promise of Bitcoin remains compelling. It continues to attract attention from investors, technologists, and financial experts who see its potential to transform the financial landscape. The ongoing development of the Bitcoin ecosystem, including advancements in blockchain technology and the introduction of regulatory frameworks, aims to address some of the issues that have plagued its early years.

Bitcoin's promise extends beyond being just a digital currency. It represents a new paradigm in financial systems, one that is decentralized, transparent, and secure. It offers a glimpse into a future where individuals have greater control over their financial transactions, free from the intermediaries that have traditionally dominated the financial sector. As Bitcoin continues to evolve, its promise of a more equitable and transparent financial system remains a powerful and transformative idea.

Early Optimism vs. Market Reality

When Bitcoin was introduced, it was heralded as a groundbreaking innovation that promised to revolutionize the financial system. The early days of Bitcoin were marked by immense optimism and enthusiasm. Proponents of the cryptocurrency believed it would provide a decentralized, transparent, and secure alternative to traditional currencies and financial systems. Bitcoin was seen as a tool to empower individuals, reduce the influence of central banks, and offer a new form of financial freedom.

The optimism surrounding Bitcoin was fueled by its underlying technology, blockchain, which offered unparalleled security and transparency. Blockchain technology ensured that every transaction was recorded on a public ledger, making it nearly impossible to alter or falsify data. This transparency was expected to build trust among users and reduce the need for intermediaries, such as banks and financial institutions. The fixed supply of Bitcoin, capped at 21 million, was designed to prevent inflation and maintain the currency's value over time.

As Bitcoin gained popularity, early adopters envisioned a future where it would be widely accepted for everyday transactions, from buying coffee to paying for online services. Businesses began to accept Bitcoin as a form of payment, and the media was filled with stories of individuals who had made significant profits from investing in the cryptocurrency. This wave of optimism led to a surge in demand for Bitcoin, driving its price to unprecedented heights.

However, the reality of Bitcoin's market behavior soon began to diverge from the early expectations. Despite its promise of stability and security, Bitcoin became known for its extreme volatility. The price of Bitcoin experienced dramatic swings, sometimes within hours, leading to significant gains and losses for investors. This volatility was often driven by speculation, market sentiment, and external events, such as regulatory announcements or technological developments.

The disparity between early optimism and market reality became more apparent as instances of market manipulation and speculative behavior surfaced. Large holders of Bitcoin, known as "whales," were found to have a significant influence on the market. These whales could manipulate prices through coordinated buying and selling, creating artificial demand or supply. Such actions led to price spikes and crashes, further exacerbating Bitcoin's volatility.

As Bitcoin's popularity grew, so did the number of speculative investors looking to profit from its price movements. This influx of speculative capital contributed to the formation of price bubbles, which eventually burst, causing sharp declines in value. The speculative nature of the market made it difficult for Bitcoin to establish itself as a stable and reliable currency for everyday transactions.

The early optimism surrounding Bitcoin also faced challenges from regulatory bodies worldwide. Governments and financial regulators began to scrutinize the cryptocurrency market, concerned about issues such as money laundering, tax evasion, and consumer protection. Regulatory actions and statements often led to significant price movements, adding another layer of volatility to the market.

Despite these challenges, the fundamental promise of Bitcoin as a decentralized and transparent financial system remains compelling. While the market reality has exposed vulnerabilities and highlighted the need for regulatory oversight, it has also spurred innovation and development within the cryptocurrency ecosystem. The lessons learned from Bitcoin's early years continue to shape the future of digital currencies, driving efforts to create more stable and secure alternatives.

In conclusion, the journey of Bitcoin from early optimism to market reality underscores the complexities and challenges inherent in pioneering a new financial paradigm. While the initial promise of Bitcoin has been tempered by market volatility and speculative behavior, it has also sparked a global conversation about the future of money and finance. As the cryptocurrency market evolves, it is essential to address these challenges and build a more robust and sustainable ecosystem that fulfills the original vision of decentralization, transparency, and financial empowerment.

A Call for Investigation

The emergence of Bitcoin has been accompanied by a wave of optimism and subsequent disillusionment as market realities diverged sharply from initial expectations. While the cryptocurrency promised a decentralized and transparent financial system, it quickly became apparent that the market was susceptible to manipulation and volatility. This discrepancy between Bitcoin's theoretical benefits and practical challenges underscores the need for a thorough investigation into the factors driving its price fluctuations and the behavior of its market participants.

Bitcoin was introduced with the revolutionary vision of providing an alternative to the centralized financial systems that dominate the global economy. Its decentralized nature and the transparency of blockchain technology were designed to eliminate the need for intermediaries, reduce transaction costs, and protect against inflation through a fixed supply of 21 million Bitcoins. However, the reality of Bitcoin's market behavior has exposed significant vulnerabilities, particularly its extreme volatility and susceptibility to manipulation by powerful market players.

The market dynamics of Bitcoin are influenced by several factors, including speculation, regulatory actions, and the activities of large holders known as "whales." These whales, by controlling substantial portions of the Bitcoin supply, have the ability to manipulate prices through coordinated buying and selling. This manipulation creates artificial market conditions, leading to sudden price spikes and crashes that can result in significant financial losses for smaller investors. The tools and strategies employed by these manipulators, such as wash trading and pump-and-dump schemes, further exacerbate market volatility and undermine the integrity of the Bitcoin market.

The volatility of Bitcoin and its susceptibility to manipulation raise critical questions about its viability as a stable financial asset. Despite its promise of decentralization and transparency, the concentration of power in the hands of a few large players contradicts the very principles Bitcoin was meant to uphold. This centralization of influence can erode trust in the cryptocurrency market, deter new investors, and stifle innovation. Moreover, the lack of regulatory oversight allows manipulative practices to thrive, further undermining the stability and credibility of the market.

Given these challenges, it is imperative to conduct a thorough investigation into the factors driving Bitcoin's price volatility and the behavior of its market participants. This investigation should focus on identifying and addressing the manipulative practices that distort the natural supply and demand dynamics of the market. By shedding light on these practices, we can better understand the underlying causes of Bitcoin's volatility and develop strategies to mitigate their impact.

The broader implications of this investigation extend beyond the Bitcoin market itself. They highlight the urgent need for regulatory measures to address market manipulation and foster a more transparent and stable market environment. Effective regulation can help protect investors, promote market integrity, and ensure the long-term sustainability of Bitcoin and other cryptocurrencies.

Moreover, this investigation can provide valuable insights for traders and investors, helping them recognize the signs of market manipulation and make more informed decisions. By staying vigilant and employing risk management strategies, market participants can navigate the complexities of the Bitcoin market and mitigate potential losses. The push for greater transparency and regulatory oversight can contribute to a healthier and more sustainable cryptocurrency ecosystem, ultimately benefiting all stakeholders.

In conclusion, the discrepancy between the early optimism surrounding Bitcoin and the market reality underscores the need for a thorough investigation into its market dynamics. By addressing the manipulative practices that drive its volatility, we can better understand the challenges facing Bitcoin and develop strategies to realize its original promise of a decentralized, transparent, and fair financial system. This investigation is not only essential for protecting investors and promoting market integrity but also for ensuring the future of Bitcoin and its role in the global financial landscape.

Chapter 1: Understanding Bitcoin's Design and Structure

The Fundamentals of Bitcoin

What is Bitcoin?

Bitcoin is a form of digital currency that was created in 2009 by an anonymous individual or group of individuals using the pseudonym Satoshi Nakamoto. Unlike traditional currencies issued by governments and central banks, Bitcoin operates on a decentralized network using peer-to-peer technology, allowing users to transact directly without intermediaries. This decentralization is one of the core principles that distinguish Bitcoin from traditional financial systems.

At the heart of Bitcoin is blockchain technology, a distributed ledger that records all transactions across a network of computers. This ledger is public and transparent, meaning that anyone can view the transaction history, which helps to prevent fraud and ensure the integrity of the system. Each block in the blockchain contains a list of transactions, and these blocks are linked together in chronological order, forming a chain. Once a block is added to the blockchain, the information it contains cannot be altered, making the system secure and immutable.

Bitcoin is created through a process called mining, which involves using powerful computers to solve complex mathematical problems. Miners compete to solve these problems, and the first one to find a solution is rewarded with a certain number of new Bitcoins. This process not only generates new Bitcoins but also secures the network by verifying and recording transactions. The total supply of Bitcoin is capped at 21 million, a feature designed to mimic the scarcity of precious metals like gold and to prevent inflation.

One of the key features of Bitcoin is its decentralized nature. Unlike traditional currencies, which are controlled by central banks, Bitcoin is maintained by a network of nodes operated by volunteers around the world. These nodes validate transactions and ensure the integrity of the blockchain. This decentralized structure means that no single entity has control over the Bitcoin network, making it resistant to censorship and centralized manipulation.

Bitcoin transactions are pseudonymous, meaning that they are not directly linked to real-world identities. Instead, users transact using addresses, which are long strings of alphanumeric characters. While this provides a certain level of privacy, it is important to note that all transactions are recorded on the public blockchain, and it is possible to trace the flow of Bitcoins between addresses.

One of the primary use cases for Bitcoin is as a digital store of value. Due to its limited supply and decentralized nature, Bitcoin is often referred to as "digital gold." Investors see it as a hedge against inflation and a way to preserve wealth over the long term. Additionally, Bitcoin can be used for online purchases, remittances, and other types of transactions, although its price volatility can sometimes make it less practical for everyday use.

The introduction of Bitcoin has sparked a wave of innovation in the financial sector. It has led to the development of numerous other cryptocurrencies and blockchain-based projects, collectively known as the cryptocurrency ecosystem. This ecosystem includes various platforms for trading, investing, and using digital assets, as well as decentralized applications (dApps) that offer a wide range of services.

Despite its potential, Bitcoin faces several challenges. Its price is highly volatile, and it has been subject to significant fluctuations over short periods. This volatility can be attributed to various factors, including speculative trading, market manipulation, regulatory uncertainty, and technological developments. Additionally, the scalability of the Bitcoin network has been a topic of ongoing debate, with concerns about transaction speeds and fees as the number of users grows.

In conclusion, Bitcoin is a pioneering digital currency that operates on a decentralized network using blockchain technology. It offers a secure, transparent, and efficient way to transfer value without the need for intermediaries. While it holds significant promise as a digital store of value and a medium of exchange, it also faces challenges related to volatility, scalability, and regulatory scrutiny. Understanding what Bitcoin is and how it works is crucial for anyone interested in the evolving landscape of digital finance.

The Blockchain Technology

Blockchain technology is the foundation upon which Bitcoin and many other cryptocurrencies are built. It is a decentralized and distributed digital ledger that records transactions across many computers in such a way that the registered transactions cannot be altered retroactively. This ensures the integrity and security of the data without the need for a central authority. The innovation of blockchain technology lies in its ability to provide a trustworthy and tamper-proof system for recording transactions.

At its core, a blockchain is composed of blocks, each containing a list of transactions. These blocks are linked together in chronological order through cryptographic hashes, forming a chain. Each block contains a unique code known as a hash, which not only identifies the block but also links it to the previous block. This interconnected structure ensures that any attempt to alter a transaction would require changing all subsequent blocks, an effort that is practically impossible due to the immense computational power required.

The process of adding a new block to the blockchain is called mining. Miners use powerful computers to solve complex mathematical problems that validate transactions and add them to the blockchain. This process, known as proof of work, requires significant computational effort, ensuring that only legitimate transactions are added to the blockchain. Once a block is added, it is propagated across the entire network of nodes, making it virtually immutable.

Blockchain technology offers several key advantages that make it suitable for applications beyond cryptocurrency. Its decentralized nature means that no single entity has control over the entire network, reducing the risk of censorship or manipulation. The transparency of the blockchain allows anyone to verify transactions independently, fostering trust among users. Additionally, the security provided by cryptographic hashing and the distributed nature of the network makes blockchain highly resistant to fraud and cyberattacks.

One of the most significant contributions of blockchain technology is its potential to revolutionize various industries by providing a secure and transparent way to record transactions. In finance, blockchain can streamline processes such as cross-border payments, clearing, and settlement, reducing costs and increasing efficiency. In supply chain management, blockchain can enhance traceability, ensuring that products are authentic and sourced responsibly. The healthcare industry can benefit from blockchain by securing patient records and enabling seamless data sharing between providers while maintaining patient privacy.

Smart contracts are another innovation enabled by blockchain technology. These are self-executing contracts with the terms of the agreement directly written into code. Smart contracts automatically enforce and execute the terms of a contract when predefined conditions are met, eliminating the need for intermediaries and reducing the risk of human error or fraud. Platforms like Ethereum have popularized smart contracts, allowing developers to create decentralized applications (dApps) that run on the blockchain.

Despite its transformative potential, blockchain technology faces several challenges. One of the primary concerns is scalability. The process of validating and adding transactions to the blockchain is resource-intensive and time-consuming, limiting the number of transactions that can be processed per second. Various solutions, such as sharding and layer-two protocols, are being explored to address these scalability issues and improve the efficiency of blockchain networks.

Another challenge is the regulatory environment surrounding blockchain technology and cryptocurrencies. Governments and regulatory bodies around the world are grappling with how to classify and regulate these new technologies. Clear and consistent regulations are necessary to protect consumers, prevent illicit activities, and provide a stable environment for innovation and investment.

In conclusion, blockchain technology is a groundbreaking innovation that underpins Bitcoin and has the potential to transform numerous industries. Its decentralized, transparent, and secure nature makes it an ideal solution for recording transactions and building trust in a digital world. While challenges such as scalability and regulation need to be addressed, the continued development and adoption of blockchain technology promise to unlock new possibilities and drive significant advancements in various sectors. Understanding the intricacies of blockchain is essential for anyone interested in the future of digital finance and decentralized systems.

The 21 Million Cap

A fundamental aspect of Bitcoin that sets it apart from traditional currencies is its fixed supply cap of 21 million coins. This cap, hardcoded into the Bitcoin protocol by its creator Satoshi Nakamoto, was designed to address some of the most pressing issues associated with fiat currencies, such as inflation and monetary policy manipulation. By establishing a finite supply, Bitcoin aims to create a deflationary currency model, where the value of the currency could theoretically increase over time as demand rises and supply remains limited.

The concept of a fixed supply cap introduces a stark contrast to the traditional fiat system where central banks can print money at will, leading to inflation and the devaluation of currency. Historically, the ability to print unlimited amounts of money has resulted in periods of hyperinflation, economic instability, and loss of purchasing power for individuals holding that currency. Bitcoin's finite supply is intended to mitigate these risks, providing a stable store of value over the long term.

The mechanism through which new Bitcoins are introduced into the system is known as mining. Mining is the process by which transactions are verified and added to the blockchain. Miners use computational power to solve complex mathematical puzzles, and in return, they are rewarded with newly minted Bitcoins. This process not only secures the network but also regulates the introduction of new Bitcoins into circulation. The reward for mining new blocks halves approximately every four years, in an event known as the halving. This built-in mechanism ensures that the rate of new Bitcoin creation decreases over time, gradually approaching the 21 million cap.

The impact of the 21 million cap extends beyond the technical and economic realms, influencing the perception and behavior of market participants. Investors and enthusiasts often view Bitcoin as "digital gold" because of its scarcity and deflationary properties. This perception drives a significant portion of the demand for Bitcoin, with many seeing it as a hedge against inflation and a safe haven asset in times of economic uncertainty. The fixed supply creates a sense of scarcity, which can drive up the value of Bitcoin as more people seek to acquire a piece of this limited resource.

However, the finite supply of Bitcoin also presents certain challenges and considerations. One such challenge is the potential for increased price volatility. As the total supply becomes more limited and the rate of new coin creation slows, market fluctuations can become more pronounced. Large holders, often referred to as whales, can significantly impact the market by buying or selling substantial amounts of Bitcoin, leading to sharp price movements. This volatility can pose risks for investors and complicates Bitcoin's use as a stable medium of exchange.

Additionally, the fixed supply cap raises questions about the long-term sustainability of the Bitcoin network, particularly in terms of mining incentives. As the mining rewards continue to halve and eventually cease, miners will need to rely solely on transaction fees for their income. This transition could impact the security and efficiency of the network, as miners might find it less profitable to continue their operations. Ensuring that transaction fees remain sufficient to incentivize miners without deterring users is a delicate balance that the Bitcoin community will need to address.

Furthermore, the deflationary nature of Bitcoin may have broader economic implications. In a deflationary environment, individuals might be incentivized to hoard Bitcoin rather than spend it, anticipating that its value will increase over time. This behavior could reduce liquidity and limit Bitcoin's effectiveness as a medium of exchange. Striking a balance between maintaining Bitcoin's value as a store of wealth and encouraging its use in everyday transactions is an ongoing challenge for the ecosystem.

In conclusion, the 21 million cap is a defining feature of Bitcoin that differentiates it from traditional fiat currencies and underpins its appeal as a deflationary, scarce asset. While it offers advantages in terms of protecting against inflation and providing a stable store of value, it also introduces complexities related to market volatility, mining incentives, and economic behavior. Understanding the implications of this fixed supply is crucial for anyone interested in the dynamics of Bitcoin and its potential role in the future of finance.

The Market Dynamics of Bitcoin

Supply and Demand Basics

The principles of supply and demand are fundamental to understanding the market dynamics of Bitcoin. In the context of Bitcoin, supply refers to the total number of Bitcoins available in the market, while demand represents the desire of investors and users to acquire Bitcoin. The interaction between these two forces determines the price of Bitcoin at any given time, much like it does with traditional commodities and assets.

The supply of Bitcoin is unique due to its fixed cap of 21 million coins. This finite supply is gradually released into the market through a process known as mining, where new Bitcoins are created as rewards for miners who validate transactions on the blockchain. This process of distribution is predictable and follows a pre-set schedule, with the reward for mining new blocks halving approximately every four years. As a result, the rate at which new Bitcoins are introduced into the market decreases over time, which contrasts with fiat currencies that can be printed in unlimited quantities by central banks.

On the demand side, several factors influence the desire to acquire Bitcoin. One significant factor is Bitcoin's potential as a store of value, often likened to digital gold. Investors seeking to hedge against inflation and economic instability are drawn to Bitcoin due to its scarcity and deflationary nature. Additionally, the growing acceptance of Bitcoin as a medium of exchange and its integration into financial systems and services enhance its demand. Technological advancements, such as improvements in transaction speed and scalability, also contribute to increasing demand by making Bitcoin more practical for everyday use.

Market sentiment plays a crucial role in the demand for Bitcoin. Positive news, such as regulatory approval, institutional adoption, or technological innovations, can boost investor confidence and drive up demand. Conversely, negative news, including regulatory crackdowns, security breaches, or macroeconomic uncertainties, can dampen demand and lead to price declines. The speculative nature of the market means that psychological factors and herd behavior often amplify these effects, leading to significant price volatility.

The balance between supply and demand is further complicated by the actions of large holders, known as whales. These individuals or entities hold substantial amounts of Bitcoin and can influence the market by strategically buying or selling large quantities. When whales decide to sell significant portions of their holdings, it can flood the market with supply, driving down prices. Conversely, when they accumulate Bitcoin, it can create a perception of increased demand, pushing prices higher. The strategies employed by these market participants can create artificial supply and demand dynamics, contributing to the volatility for which Bitcoin is known.

Another layer of complexity in the supply and demand dynamics of Bitcoin is the impact of mining activities. As the mining rewards halve and the total supply approaches its cap, miners may face increased operational costs without corresponding increases in revenue from newly minted Bitcoins. This could lead to shifts in mining power distribution, changes in transaction fees, and variations in the security and efficiency of the network. The anticipation of these changes can influence market sentiment and, consequently, the demand for Bitcoin.

In addition to these factors, external economic conditions and broader financial markets also play a role in shaping the supply and demand for Bitcoin. During times of economic uncertainty or financial market instability, investors may seek refuge in alternative assets like Bitcoin, increasing its demand. On the other hand, during periods of economic stability and strong performance in traditional markets, the appeal of Bitcoin as an alternative investment may wane, reducing demand.

In conclusion, the basics of supply and demand are essential to understanding the price movements of Bitcoin. The fixed supply cap, the predictable distribution of new Bitcoins, and the various factors influencing demand all interplay to create a dynamic market environment. The actions of large holders, mining activities, market sentiment, and broader economic conditions add layers of complexity to these fundamental principles. By comprehending these dynamics, investors and market participants can better navigate the volatility and opportunities presented by the Bitcoin market.

Bitcoin as Digital Gold

Bitcoin has often been referred to as "digital gold," a term that encapsulates its perceived value as a store of wealth and a hedge against economic uncertainty. This comparison arises from several similarities between Bitcoin and physical gold, particularly their scarcity, decentralized nature, and the role they play in diversifying investment portfolios.

The most obvious similarity between Bitcoin and gold is their limited supply. Gold is a finite resource, extracted from the earth in limited quantities, which contributes to its enduring value over millennia. Similarly, Bitcoin's supply is capped at 21 million coins, ensuring that no more can ever be created. This scarcity is fundamental to Bitcoin's value proposition, as it creates an intrinsic sense of worth and a hedge against inflation, much like gold.

Bitcoin's decentralized nature also mirrors that of gold. Gold has historically been valuable not because it is issued or backed by any single government, but because it is universally recognized as valuable across different cultures and economies. Bitcoin operates on a decentralized network, free from the control of any single entity or government. This decentralization ensures that Bitcoin, like gold, is not subject to the same inflationary pressures or political risks that can affect fiat currencies.

Another key factor in the comparison is the role of Bitcoin as a store of value. For centuries, gold has been used to preserve wealth, particularly during times of economic instability or geopolitical uncertainty. Investors turn to gold as a safe haven asset, confident that it will retain its value even when other investments falter. Bitcoin is increasingly being viewed in a similar light. Its proponents argue that Bitcoin provides a reliable store of value, insulated from the devaluation risks associated with fiat currencies and the volatility of stock markets.

Bitcoin's digital nature offers additional advantages over gold, particularly in terms of portability and divisibility. While gold is tangible and must be physically stored and transported, Bitcoin exists in a digital form, allowing it to be transferred quickly and easily across the globe. This makes Bitcoin exceptionally liquid and accessible, regardless of the geographical location of the owner. Furthermore, Bitcoin can be divided into smaller units, known as satoshis, making it practical for both large transactions and microtransactions. This divisibility enhances its utility as a medium of exchange, beyond its role as a store of value.

The technological underpinning of Bitcoin, its blockchain, adds another layer of security and transparency that gold cannot match. Every Bitcoin transaction is recorded on a public ledger, ensuring transparency and traceability. This immutable record reduces the risk of fraud and enhances trust among users. While gold has to be assayed and authenticated, Bitcoin's authenticity is inherent in its blockchain technology.

Despite these advantages, Bitcoin as digital gold is not without its challenges and criticisms. One of the most significant issues is its volatility. While gold prices can fluctuate, the extent and frequency of Bitcoin's price swings are far greater. This volatility can undermine its reliability as a store of value, making it a risky investment for those looking for stability. Moreover, while gold has a long history of being universally accepted as a store of value, Bitcoin is still in the relatively early stages of gaining widespread acceptance and trust.

Another concern is regulatory uncertainty. Gold is universally recognized and regulated, whereas Bitcoin's regulatory environment is still evolving. Different countries have different approaches to Bitcoin, ranging from outright bans to enthusiastic adoption. This inconsistency can affect its price and usability, adding another layer of risk for investors.

Environmental impact is another area where Bitcoin faces criticism. The process of mining Bitcoin, which involves solving complex mathematical problems to validate transactions, requires substantial computational power and energy consumption. This has raised concerns about the environmental sustainability of Bitcoin, especially when compared to gold, which, while also resource-intensive to mine, does not have the same ongoing energy requirements.

In conclusion, Bitcoin's role as digital gold highlights its potential as a store of value and a hedge against economic uncertainty, much like physical gold. Its limited supply, decentralized nature, and technological advantages make it a compelling alternative to traditional assets. However, its volatility, regulatory challenges, and environmental impact are significant factors that need to be considered. Understanding these dynamics is crucial for investors looking to navigate the evolving landscape of digital assets and harness the potential of Bitcoin as a modern-day store of wealth.

Market Participants

Understanding the Bitcoin market requires a deep dive into the diverse array of participants that influence its dynamics. The Bitcoin market is a complex ecosystem composed of various actors, each with their motivations, strategies, and levels of influence. These participants range from individual retail investors to large institutional players, miners, and a unique group known as whales, whose substantial holdings can significantly sway the market.

Retail investors form the backbone of the Bitcoin market. These individuals purchase Bitcoin through exchanges, often motivated by the prospect of high returns on investment, the allure of participating in a revolutionary financial system, or the desire to hedge against traditional financial uncertainties. Retail investors tend to have smaller holdings compared to institutional investors or whales, but collectively, their actions can drive significant market movements. The behavior of retail investors is often influenced by market sentiment, media coverage, and trends, leading to rapid buying or selling in response to perceived opportunities or threats.

Institutional investors have increasingly entered the Bitcoin market, bringing with them substantial capital and a level of legitimacy that has helped Bitcoin gain acceptance in mainstream finance. These participants include hedge funds, asset managers, and publicly traded companies that allocate a portion of their portfolios to Bitcoin. Institutional investors typically employ sophisticated trading strategies and risk management practices, contributing to the market's liquidity and stability. Their involvement has also spurred the development of financial products like Bitcoin futures and exchange-traded funds (ETFs), further integrating Bitcoin into the traditional financial system.

Miners play a crucial role in the Bitcoin ecosystem by securing the network and validating transactions. They use powerful computers to solve complex mathematical problems, a process known as proof of work. In return, they are rewarded with newly minted Bitcoins. The actions of miners can impact the market, particularly around events such as Bitcoin halving, when the reward for mining new blocks is halved. These events reduce the rate at which new Bitcoins are introduced into the market, potentially increasing scarcity and influencing price dynamics. The geographical distribution of mining operations, energy consumption, and regulatory environment also affect miners' decisions and, consequently, the market.

Whales are a distinct category of market participants characterized by their substantial Bitcoin holdings. These individuals or entities possess enough Bitcoin to influence market prices through their trading activities. Whales can impact the market by making large trades that create significant supply or demand, leading to price fluctuations. Their strategies often involve buying large amounts of Bitcoin when prices are low and selling when prices rise, maximizing their profits. The actions of whales can create volatility and uncertainty, particularly for smaller investors who may be caught off guard by sudden market shifts.

Market makers are another important group in the Bitcoin ecosystem. These participants provide liquidity to the market by continuously buying and selling Bitcoin, enabling other traders to execute orders more easily. Market makers profit from the spread between the bid and ask prices and help maintain market stability by reducing price gaps and ensuring smoother trading operations. Their activities contribute to a more efficient market, allowing for better price discovery and reduced volatility.

Speculators also play a significant role in the Bitcoin market. These participants trade Bitcoin with the primary goal of profiting from short-term price movements. Speculators include both retail investors and professional traders who use various strategies, such as technical analysis, leverage, and algorithmic trading, to capitalize on market volatility. While speculation can lead to increased liquidity, it can also contribute to excessive volatility and market bubbles, as speculative buying and selling can amplify price swings.

The media and information platforms are influential, albeit indirectly, in shaping the behavior of market participants. News outlets, social media, and financial analysts can significantly impact market sentiment by disseminating information, rumors, or analysis about Bitcoin. Positive news, such as regulatory approval or institutional adoption, can drive up demand and prices, while negative news, such as security breaches or regulatory crackdowns, can lead to panic selling and price drops. Information asymmetry, where some participants have access to information before others, can also create opportunities for manipulation and unequal advantages in the market.

In conclusion, the Bitcoin market is a dynamic and multifaceted ecosystem influenced by a diverse array of participants. Retail investors, institutional investors, miners, whales, market makers, speculators, and media platforms all play crucial roles in shaping the market's behavior and price dynamics. Understanding the motivations and strategies of these participants is essential for navigating the complexities of the Bitcoin market and making informed investment decisions. As the market continues to evolve, the interplay between these different actors will remain a key factor in determining Bitcoin's future trajectory.

Challenges in Bitcoin Valuation

Price Discovery Mechanisms

In the world of Bitcoin, the concept of price discovery plays a critical role in determining the value of the cryptocurrency. Price discovery refers to the process by which the market determines the price of an asset through the interactions of buyers and sellers. This mechanism is essential for understanding how the market evaluates Bitcoin at any given moment, reflecting the collective sentiment, supply and demand dynamics, and external influences.

Bitcoin's price discovery primarily occurs on cryptocurrency exchanges. These platforms act as marketplaces where individuals and institutions can buy and sell Bitcoin. The most popular exchanges, such as Coinbase, Binance, and Kraken, see significant trading volumes, making them central to the price discovery process. The price at which a Bitcoin is traded on these exchanges represents the consensus of its value among the participating market players at that particular time.

A key factor in Bitcoin's price discovery is market liquidity, which refers to the ease with which an asset can be bought or sold without causing significant price changes. High liquidity is indicative of a healthy market where there are enough buyers and sellers to facilitate smooth transactions. In contrast, low liquidity can lead to increased volatility, as large orders can disproportionately impact the price. The liquidity of Bitcoin can vary across different exchanges and times of day, influencing the price discovery process.

The order book on an exchange is a fundamental tool in the price discovery process. It lists the buy and sell orders placed by traders, showing the quantities they are willing to trade at specific prices. The bid price represents the highest price a buyer is willing to pay, while the ask price is the lowest price a seller is willing to accept. The gap between these two prices, known as the bid-ask spread, provides insights into market liquidity and trader sentiment. A narrower spread typically indicates higher liquidity and more active trading, facilitating more accurate price discovery.

Another important aspect of Bitcoin's price discovery is trading volume. Higher trading volumes generally lead to more reliable price discovery because they reflect a larger number of transactions and a greater diversity of market participants. Volume can also signal the strength of a price movement; for instance, a price increase accompanied by high volume is often seen as more sustainable than one with low volume, as it suggests broader market support.

Arbitrage opportunities also play a role in price discovery. Arbitrage involves taking advantage of price differences for the same asset across different markets or exchanges. For example, if Bitcoin is priced lower on one exchange compared to another, traders may buy on the cheaper exchange and sell on the more expensive one. This process helps align prices across different platforms, contributing to a more uniform and accurate reflection of Bitcoin's value.

Futures and derivative markets are increasingly influential in Bitcoin's price discovery. Platforms like the Chicago Mercantile Exchange (CME) offer Bitcoin futures contracts, allowing traders to speculate on the future price of Bitcoin. These markets can impact the spot price of Bitcoin, as the expectations and sentiments reflected in futures contracts influence buying and selling decisions in the spot market. Additionally, options markets, where traders can buy and sell contracts giving them the right to trade Bitcoin at specific prices, further contribute to the complex landscape of price discovery.

Market sentiment and external factors also significantly affect Bitcoin's price discovery. News events, regulatory developments, technological advancements, and macroeconomic trends can all influence market behavior. Positive news, such as a major company adopting Bitcoin or favorable regulatory changes, can drive up demand and prices. Conversely, negative news, such as security breaches or regulatory crackdowns, can lead to panic selling and price drops. Social media platforms and forums, where traders and investors discuss market trends and share opinions, also play a role in shaping market sentiment and influencing price discovery.

Lastly, the role of large market participants, often referred to as whales, cannot be overlooked in the price discovery process. Whales, with their substantial Bitcoin holdings, can significantly influence market prices through large buy or sell orders. Their actions can create short-term price volatility, impacting the overall process of price discovery. The strategies employed by these players, including strategic buying or selling and market manipulation techniques, can distort the natural supply and demand dynamics, complicating the accurate determination of Bitcoin's value.

In conclusion, the price discovery mechanisms for Bitcoin involve a complex interplay of market liquidity, trading volume, order books, arbitrage opportunities, futures and derivatives markets, market sentiment, external factors, and the actions of large market participants. Understanding these mechanisms is crucial for anyone looking to navigate the Bitcoin market, as they provide insights into how the value of Bitcoin is determined and the factors that can influence its price at any given time.

Volatility Factors

The volatility of Bitcoin is a defining characteristic that has both attracted and repelled investors since its inception. Understanding the factors that contribute to this volatility is crucial for anyone looking to navigate the Bitcoin market. Several key elements drive the price fluctuations of Bitcoin, including market sentiment, regulatory developments, technological advancements, macroeconomic factors, and the actions of large holders known as whales.

Market sentiment plays a significant role in Bitcoin's volatility. The cryptocurrency market is heavily influenced by news and events that can swiftly change investor perceptions. Positive developments, such as major companies adopting Bitcoin or regulatory approvals, can lead to sharp price increases as optimism and confidence surge. Conversely, negative news, such as regulatory crackdowns, security breaches, or significant market sell-offs, can trigger panic and lead to steep price declines. The psychological impact of these events often results in exaggerated market movements, contributing to Bitcoin's overall volatility.

Regulatory developments are another critical factor influencing Bitcoin's price volatility. The regulatory environment for cryptocurrencies is still evolving, with different countries adopting varied approaches. Announcements of new regulations or government actions can lead to significant market reactions. For instance, news of potential bans on cryptocurrency trading or mining in major markets can cause fear and uncertainty, prompting sell-offs and driving prices down. Conversely, regulatory clarity and supportive policies can enhance market confidence and drive prices up.

Technological advancements and innovations within the Bitcoin ecosystem also impact its volatility. Upgrades to the Bitcoin network, such as improvements in scalability, transaction speed, and security, can enhance the cryptocurrency's utility and attractiveness, leading to increased demand and price appreciation. However, technological issues, such as network congestion or vulnerabilities, can erode confidence and result in price declines. Additionally, developments in related technologies, such as the rise of decentralized finance (DeFi) or advancements in blockchain interoperability, can influence Bitcoin's market dynamics.

Macroeconomic factors, including global economic conditions and monetary policies, play a significant role in Bitcoin's price movements. During periods of economic uncertainty or financial instability, investors often seek alternative assets to preserve their wealth, leading to increased demand for Bitcoin as a hedge against traditional financial markets. For example, during the COVID-19 pandemic, the unprecedented monetary stimulus measures by central banks led to fears of inflation, driving more investors towards Bitcoin. Conversely, strong performance in traditional markets or tightening monetary policies can reduce Bitcoin's appeal as an alternative investment, leading to price declines.

The actions of large holders, known as whales, have a profound impact on Bitcoin's volatility. These entities, which hold significant amounts of Bitcoin, can influence market prices through their trading activities. When whales decide to buy or sell large quantities of Bitcoin, they can create substantial supply or demand, leading to sharp price movements. The strategies employed by whales, including coordinated buying and selling, can amplify volatility and create market distortions. Their actions can also trigger panic or euphoria among smaller investors, further exacerbating price swings.

Speculation and trading activities add another layer of volatility to the Bitcoin market. Many investors and traders are drawn to Bitcoin for its potential to generate high returns over short periods. This speculative behavior leads to frequent buying and selling, contributing to price fluctuations. High leverage trading, where traders borrow funds to amplify their positions, can also intensify volatility. Liquidations of leveraged positions during price swings can create a cascade effect, driving prices further in the direction of the initial movement.

Market manipulation tactics, such as pump-and-dump schemes and wash trading, also contribute to Bitcoin's volatility. These deceptive practices create artificial market activity and can lead to sudden and significant price changes. For example, pump-and-dump schemes involve artificially inflating the price of Bitcoin through coordinated buying, followed by a rapid sell-off to profit from the price spike, leaving other investors with losses. Wash trading, where traders simultaneously buy and sell Bitcoin to create misleading volume and price movements, further distorts the market and contributes to volatility.

In conclusion, the volatility of Bitcoin is driven by a complex interplay of factors, including market sentiment, regulatory developments, technological advancements, macroeconomic conditions, the actions of whales, speculative trading, and market manipulation. Understanding these factors is essential for investors and traders to navigate the Bitcoin market effectively. While volatility presents risks, it also offers opportunities for those who can anticipate and respond to market movements. As the Bitcoin market continues to mature, efforts to address these volatility factors through regulatory measures, technological improvements, and market education will be crucial in fostering a more stable and sustainable ecosystem.

Real vs. Perceived Value

The distinction between real and perceived value in Bitcoin is a complex and multifaceted issue that influences its market behavior and overall valuation. Real value refers to the intrinsic worth of an asset based on tangible factors such as utility, scarcity, and production costs. Perceived value, on the other hand, is shaped by market sentiment, investor psychology, and speculative interests. The interplay between these two types of value is crucial in understanding the dynamics of Bitcoin's market price.

Bitcoin's real value is often debated among economists, investors, and technologists. One of the key components of its real value is its utility as a decentralized digital currency. Bitcoin allows for peer-to-peer transactions without the need for intermediaries, such as banks or payment processors. This utility is particularly valuable in regions with unstable financial systems or where access to traditional banking services is limited. Additionally, Bitcoin's blockchain technology ensures secure, transparent, and immutable transactions, further enhancing its real value as a reliable digital asset.

Scarcity is another fundamental aspect of Bitcoin's real value. The finite supply cap of 21 million Bitcoins introduces a level of scarcity similar to precious metals like gold. As the supply of new Bitcoins diminishes over time through the halving process, the scarcity factor is expected to drive up its value, assuming constant or increasing demand. This scarcity is integral to Bitcoin's appeal as a store of value and a hedge against inflation, positioning it as "digital gold."

Production costs also contribute to Bitcoin's real value. Mining Bitcoin requires significant computational power and energy, resulting in substantial costs for miners. These costs include hardware investments, electricity, and maintenance expenses. The difficulty of mining adjusts periodically to maintain a consistent block production rate, ensuring that the effort and resources required to mine new Bitcoins reflect its value. Thus, the production cost provides a baseline for Bitcoin's real value, as miners are unlikely to sell below their cost of production over the long term.

Despite these tangible aspects of real value, Bitcoin's market price is heavily influenced by perceived value. Market sentiment, driven by news, social media, and influential figures, can cause dramatic fluctuations in Bitcoin's price. Positive news, such as endorsements by prominent investors or adoption by major companies, can boost perceived value and drive up prices. Conversely, negative news, such as regulatory crackdowns or security breaches, can diminish perceived value and lead to price declines.

Investor psychology and speculative behavior play significant roles in shaping Bitcoin's perceived value. The fear of missing out (FOMO) can drive rapid price increases as investors rush to buy Bitcoin, anticipating future gains. Conversely, fear, uncertainty, and doubt (FUD) can trigger panic selling and sharp price drops. The speculative nature of Bitcoin trading, with many investors seeking short-term profits, amplifies these psychological effects, contributing to volatility and divergence from Bitcoin's real value.

The influence of large holders, or whales, further complicates the relationship between real and perceived value. Whales can manipulate market sentiment and perceived value through strategic buying and selling. Their actions can create artificial price movements that may not align with Bitcoin's intrinsic worth. For instance, coordinated selling by whales can drive prices down, creating a perception of declining value, even if the underlying fundamentals remain strong.

Technological advancements and regulatory developments also impact Bitcoin's perceived value. Innovations that improve scalability, transaction speed, and security can enhance Bitcoin's utility and boost investor confidence, increasing perceived value. Regulatory clarity and supportive policies can similarly enhance perceived value by reducing uncertainty and legitimizing Bitcoin as a mainstream asset. Conversely, technological setbacks or regulatory hurdles can diminish perceived value and lead to price declines.

The media and information landscape significantly shape Bitcoin's perceived value. News outlets, social media platforms, and financial analysts play crucial roles in disseminating information and influencing public perception. Positive media coverage can attract new investors and increase perceived value, while negative reports can instill fear and drive prices down. The rapid spread of information, coupled with the 24/7 nature of cryptocurrency markets, means that perceived value can change quickly and dramatically based on the latest news and trends.

In conclusion, the distinction between real and perceived value is essential for understanding Bitcoin's market dynamics. While Bitcoin's real value is grounded in its utility, scarcity, and production costs, its market price is often driven by perceived value influenced by market sentiment, investor psychology, and speculative behavior. Recognizing the factors that shape both real and perceived value can help investors navigate the complexities of the Bitcoin market and make more informed decisions. As Bitcoin continues to evolve, the interplay between these two types of value will remain a critical aspect of its valuation and market behavior.

Chapter 2: The Myth of Natural Fluctuations

Analyzing Volatility

Historical Price Movements

Bitcoin's historical price movements provide a vivid illustration of its inherent volatility and the various factors that influence its value. As of today, July 21, 2024, Bitcoin is trading at $67,810.87, reflecting a 3.21% increase over the past 24 hours (CryptoExchange) (CoinDesk). This price is part of a broader trend that has seen Bitcoin reach new highs and experience significant fluctuations.

Bitcoin's journey began in 2009, but it was not until 2010 that it gained notable traction. The first real-world transaction using Bitcoin occurred in May 2010, when a programmer bought two pizzas for 10,000 Bitcoins. This transaction highlighted Bitcoin's initial obscurity and set the stage for its future price movements. By 2011, Bitcoin's price had surged from mere cents to $31, only to crash back down to $2 by the end of the year, demonstrating its early volatility.

In 2013, Bitcoin experienced two significant price bubbles. The first surge saw its price rise from $13 in January to over $266 in April, driven by increased media attention and growing adoption. This rally was followed by a sharp correction, but later in the year, Bitcoin's price skyrocketed again, surpassing $1,000 by November. These rapid price increases and subsequent corrections highlighted the speculative nature of the market.

The period between 2014 and 2016 was relatively stable compared to previous years, though it was marked by notable events like the collapse of Mt. Gox in early 2014, which temporarily dented market confidence. During this time, Bitcoin's price fluctuated between $200 and $600, laying the groundwork for the next major bull run.

The 2017 bull market is one of the most memorable periods in Bitcoin's history. Starting the year at around $1,000, Bitcoin's price surged to nearly $20,000 by December, driven by mainstream media coverage, the launch of Bitcoin futures markets, and a surge of retail investor interest. However, this dramatic rise was unsustainable, and by early 2018, Bitcoin's price had plummeted to around $6,000, eventually bottoming out at approximately $3,200 by December 2018.

The recovery phase began in 2019, with Bitcoin gradually increasing in value and reaching around $12,000 by mid-year. The onset of the COVID-19 pandemic in 2020 initially caused a sharp drop in Bitcoin's price, mirroring the broader financial markets. However, it quickly rebounded, driven by unprecedented monetary stimulus measures and increased institutional interest. By December 2020, Bitcoin had surpassed its previous all-time high, reaching $20,000.

The bull run continued into 2021, with Bitcoin peaking at over $64,000 in April. This surge was driven by institutional adoption, increased retail interest, and the perception of Bitcoin as a hedge against inflation. Nevertheless, by mid-2021, Bitcoin's price had fallen to around $30,000 due to regulatory concerns and market corrections.

In 2024, Bitcoin has experienced significant price movements, including a new all-time high of over $73,700 in March, driven by the approval of spot Bitcoin ETFs by the SEC and the halving event in April 2024. These developments have contributed to bullish market sentiment, despite ongoing regulatory challenges and market volatility.

Throughout its history, Bitcoin's price movements have been influenced by a complex interplay of technological developments, regulatory actions, market sentiment, and macroeconomic factors. This historical perspective provides valuable insights into the forces that shape Bitcoin's market and its potential future trajectory. Understanding these trends is crucial for navigating the ever-evolving landscape of Bitcoin and making informed investment decisions.

Common Explanations

The value of Bitcoin is often explained through a variety of lenses, each providing different insights into why the cryptocurrency behaves the way it does. These explanations range from fundamental economic principles to the psychological factors driving investor behavior, and they highlight the complexity of understanding Bitcoin's true nature.

One common explanation for Bitcoin's value is its utility as a decentralized digital currency. Bitcoin allows for peer-to-peer transactions without the need for intermediaries like banks or payment processors. This feature is particularly valuable in regions with unstable financial systems or where access to traditional banking is limited. By enabling secure, transparent, and low-cost transactions, Bitcoin offers a practical solution for many people around the world. Its utility in facilitating cross-border payments and acting as a store of value also contributes significantly to its perceived worth.

Another frequently cited reason for Bitcoin's value is its scarcity. Unlike fiat currencies, which can be printed in unlimited quantities by central banks, Bitcoin has a fixed supply cap of 21 million coins. This limited supply is designed to mimic the scarcity of precious metals like gold, creating an intrinsic value based on the principle of supply and demand. As more people become interested in owning Bitcoin and the supply remains capped, the price naturally tends to increase. This scarcity factor is a fundamental aspect of Bitcoin's appeal as a digital asset.

The cost of production also plays a role in determining Bitcoin's value. Bitcoin mining involves solving complex mathematical problems, which requires significant computational power and energy consumption. The expenses associated with mining, including hardware costs and electricity, set a baseline for Bitcoin's value. Miners are unlikely to sell their Bitcoin below the cost of production over the long term, as doing so would result in financial losses. This cost of production provides a floor to Bitcoin's price, ensuring that it retains some value even during market downturns.

Investor psychology and market sentiment are crucial factors in Bitcoin's price movements. The cryptocurrency market is heavily influenced by news, social media, and the actions of prominent figures in the industry. Positive news, such as regulatory approval or the adoption of Bitcoin by major companies, can drive up demand and prices. Conversely, negative news, such as security breaches or unfavorable regulatory developments, can lead to panic selling and price declines. The psychological impact of these events often results in exaggerated market reactions, contributing to Bitcoin's volatility.

Speculative trading is another key driver of Bitcoin's price. Many investors are drawn to Bitcoin not for its utility or scarcity, but for the potential of making quick profits. This speculative behavior can lead to rapid price increases as investors rush to buy Bitcoin during bullish periods, driven by the fear of missing out (FOMO). However, speculative trading can also result in sharp price drops when market sentiment shifts, as investors quickly sell off their holdings to avoid losses. This cycle of boom and bust is a characteristic feature of the cryptocurrency market.

Market manipulation by large holders, known as whales, also significantly impacts Bitcoin's price. Whales possess substantial amounts of Bitcoin and can influence market prices through strategic buying and selling. For example, a whale might buy large quantities of Bitcoin to drive up the price and then sell off their holdings at the peak, profiting from the price increase. These manipulative practices create artificial price movements that can mislead other investors and exacerbate market volatility.

Regulatory developments and government actions are important external factors that influence Bitcoin's value. The regulatory environment for cryptocurrencies is still evolving, with different countries adopting various approaches. Positive regulatory news, such as the legalization of Bitcoin in a new market or the introduction of favorable regulations, can boost investor confidence and drive up prices. Conversely, regulatory crackdowns or bans can create uncertainty and lead to price declines. The impact of regulatory actions underscores the importance of legal and policy frameworks in shaping the cryptocurrency market.

Technological advancements within the Bitcoin ecosystem also affect its value. Improvements in Bitcoin's underlying technology, such as enhancements to scalability, transaction speed, and security, can increase its utility and attractiveness to users and investors. Innovations like the Lightning Network, which aims to enable faster and cheaper transactions, contribute to Bitcoin's long-term viability and value. Technological issues or vulnerabilities, however, can negatively impact investor confidence and lead to price declines.

Macroeconomic factors, including global economic conditions and monetary policies, play a significant role in Bitcoin's valuation. During times of economic instability or financial crisis, investors often seek alternative assets like Bitcoin as a hedge against traditional financial systems. The perception of Bitcoin as "digital gold" reinforces its role as a store of value during uncertain times. Conversely, strong economic performance and stability in traditional markets can reduce the appeal of Bitcoin, leading to lower demand and prices.

In summary, the value of Bitcoin is influenced by a complex interplay of utility, scarcity, production costs, investor psychology, speculative trading, market manipulation, regulatory developments, technological advancements, and macroeconomic factors. Understanding these common explanations helps to provide a comprehensive picture of what drives Bitcoin's price and why it behaves the way it does. This multifaceted approach is essential for investors, traders, and anyone interested in the dynamics of the cryptocurrency market.

Inadequacies of Traditional Explanations

Traditional explanations for Bitcoin's price volatility often fall short in fully capturing the complexities of the cryptocurrency market. Commonly cited reasons, such as supply and demand dynamics, investor psychology, and speculative trading, provide a foundation for understanding Bitcoin's price movements but fail to account for the nuanced and multifaceted nature of its fluctuations. These traditional explanations inadequately address the deeper, systemic issues and the influence of sophisticated market manipulations that play significant roles in shaping Bitcoin's market behavior.

One of the primary inadequacies of traditional explanations is their reliance on basic economic principles of supply and demand without considering the unique characteristics of Bitcoin. Unlike traditional commodities, Bitcoin's supply is fixed at 21 million coins. While this scarcity is expected to drive value, it does not account for the dramatic price swings observed in the market. Traditional models assume a relatively stable and predictable market environment, which is seldom the case for Bitcoin. The cryptocurrency market is highly fragmented, with numerous exchanges operating independently, leading to discrepancies in liquidity and price discovery across different platforms.

Furthermore, traditional explanations often overlook the impact of market sentiment and the psychological factors driving Bitcoin's price movements. While it is acknowledged that investor behavior can influence prices, the extent to which emotions, fear, and greed dictate market actions is often underestimated. Bitcoin's market is particularly susceptible to news and events, with significant price changes occurring in response to regulatory announcements, technological developments, or influential endorsements. This heightened sensitivity to external factors amplifies volatility and is not adequately explained by conventional economic theories.

Speculative trading is another factor commonly cited in traditional explanations, but its role in Bitcoin's volatility is more profound and pervasive than in traditional markets. Bitcoin attracts a large number of speculative traders who engage in high-frequency trading, leveraging, and other strategies that can lead to rapid and extreme price movements. The speculative nature of Bitcoin trading is often fueled by the fear of missing out (FOMO) and the fear, uncertainty, and doubt (FUD) that pervade the market. These psychological triggers cause abrupt and significant shifts in market sentiment, resulting in volatile price actions that traditional models struggle to predict or explain.

Moreover, traditional explanations fail to adequately address the manipulative practices that are rampant in the Bitcoin market. Large holders, known as whales, possess the ability to influence prices through coordinated buying and selling strategies. These whales can execute large trades that create artificial demand or supply, driving prices up or down to their advantage. Techniques such as wash trading, where traders simultaneously buy and sell to create false market activity, and pump-and-dump schemes, where prices are artificially inflated and then sold off at a profit, further distort the market. These manipulative practices undermine the reliability of traditional explanations based on genuine market dynamics.

The decentralized nature of Bitcoin and the lack of regulatory oversight also contribute to its unique volatility, aspects that traditional explanations often fail to incorporate. Unlike traditional financial markets, which are subject to regulatory scrutiny and intervention, the Bitcoin market operates with minimal regulation. This regulatory vacuum allows for a higher degree of market manipulation and speculative behavior. The absence of centralized authority means that there are fewer safeguards against fraudulent activities and market abuses, leading to a more volatile and unpredictable market environment.

Additionally, technological factors unique to Bitcoin and other cryptocurrencies introduce complexities that traditional financial theories do not account for. Issues such as network congestion, transaction fees, and the scalability of the blockchain can significantly impact Bitcoin's market dynamics. Technological advancements, forks, and upgrades can lead to uncertainty and speculation, causing price fluctuations that are difficult to explain through conventional economic models.

In conclusion, while traditional explanations based on supply and demand, investor psychology, and speculative trading provide some insight into Bitcoin's price movements, they fall short of fully capturing the intricate and multifaceted nature of the cryptocurrency market. The inadequacies of these explanations lie in their failure to account for the unique characteristics of Bitcoin, the impact of manipulative practices, the decentralized and unregulated market environment, and the technological factors specific to cryptocurrencies. A deeper understanding of Bitcoin's volatility requires a comprehensive approach that considers these additional layers of complexity and the systemic issues that drive its unpredictable price behavior.

Manipulation Techniques

Pump and Dump Schemes

Pump and dump schemes are a manipulative practice that has plagued financial markets for decades, and the Bitcoin market is no exception. These schemes involve artificially inflating the price of an asset through false or misleading information, only to sell off the inflated asset at a profit, leaving unsuspecting investors with significant losses. Understanding the mechanics and impact of pump and dump schemes is crucial for navigating the volatile landscape of Bitcoin trading.

In a typical pump and dump scheme, the orchestrators first accumulate a substantial amount of the target asset, in this case, Bitcoin. This accumulation phase is conducted quietly to avoid drawing attention. Once a significant position is established, the next phase involves 'pumping' the price. This is achieved through the dissemination of positive, often misleading, information about Bitcoin. The promoters of the scheme use various channels, such as social media, online forums, and even coordinated messaging in chat groups, to create hype and excitement around Bitcoin.

As the price begins to rise due to the artificial demand generated by the promoters, more investors are drawn in by the fear of missing out (FOMO). This influx of buying pressure drives the price even higher, creating a feedback loop where rising prices attract more buyers, further pushing up the price. During this phase, the orchestrators of the scheme continue to pump up the price with ongoing positive messages and sometimes fabricated news.

Once the price reaches a sufficiently high level, the orchestrators move to the 'dump' phase. They start selling off their holdings at the inflated prices. Because they hold a large amount of Bitcoin, their selling exerts significant downward pressure on the price. As the price begins to fall, panic sets in among the other investors who were drawn into the scheme. These investors, realizing that the price is dropping rapidly, rush to sell their holdings to cut their losses, further accelerating the price decline.

The result is a rapid collapse in the price of Bitcoin, leaving many investors with substantial losses. The orchestrators, having sold at the peak, walk away with significant profits. This manipulation distorts the natural supply and demand dynamics of the market, leading to mistrust and skepticism among genuine investors.

Several factors make the Bitcoin market particularly susceptible to pump and dump schemes. Firstly, the market operates 24/7, allowing manipulators to exploit times of low trading volume, such as weekends or holidays, when fewer traders are active, and liquidity is lower. This makes it easier to influence the price with relatively small amounts of capital. Secondly, the pseudonymous nature of Bitcoin transactions and the lack of stringent regulatory oversight create an environment where it is challenging to track and prosecute perpetrators of these schemes.

The impact of pump and dump schemes extends beyond the immediate financial losses suffered by investors. These schemes undermine the integrity of the market and erode trust in Bitcoin as a legitimate asset. Repeated occurrences of such manipulative practices can deter new investors, reduce market participation, and stifle the growth and maturation of the Bitcoin ecosystem. Additionally, they contribute to the overall volatility of Bitcoin, as sudden price spikes and crashes create an unpredictable trading environment.

Addressing pump and dump schemes in the Bitcoin market requires a multifaceted approach. Increased regulatory oversight and enforcement can deter would-be manipulators by increasing the risk of detection and punishment. Exchanges can also play a crucial role by implementing stricter monitoring and controls to detect unusual trading patterns and taking proactive measures to prevent manipulation. Educating investors about the signs of pump and dump schemes and encouraging them to perform due diligence before making investment decisions can also help mitigate the impact of these schemes.

In conclusion, pump and dump schemes are a significant challenge in the Bitcoin market, exploiting the asset's inherent volatility and the decentralized, lightly regulated nature of cryptocurrency trading. Understanding how these schemes operate and recognizing the signs can help investors protect themselves from falling victim to such manipulation. Addressing these practices is essential for fostering a more transparent, stable, and trustworthy Bitcoin market, ultimately contributing to the long-term success and adoption of Bitcoin as a legitimate financial asset.

Wash Trading

Wash trading is a deceptive practice that has been prevalent in traditional financial markets and has found a fertile ground in the unregulated environment of the Bitcoin market. This practice involves simultaneously buying and selling the same financial instruments to create an illusion of market activity and manipulate prices. Understanding the mechanisms and impact of wash trading is essential for anyone navigating the volatile landscape of Bitcoin.

In the Bitcoin market, wash trading is primarily used to artificially inflate trading volumes and create misleading signals about the demand and liquidity of the cryptocurrency. Traders or entities involved in wash trading place buy and sell orders for Bitcoin simultaneously, often using multiple accounts or automated trading bots. These trades cancel each other out, resulting in no actual change in ownership, but they generate significant transaction volumes that can deceive other market participants.

The primary motivation behind wash trading in the Bitcoin market is to attract more traders by creating the appearance of high liquidity and robust market activity. High trading volumes are often associated with a healthy and active market, which can lure new investors who are looking for opportunities to buy or sell Bitcoin without facing significant price slippage. By simulating increased market activity, wash traders can draw in unsuspecting investors, driving up the price of Bitcoin through the perceived demand.

Wash trading also plays a role in price manipulation. By creating the illusion of heightened trading activity, manipulators can influence market sentiment and drive price movements in their favor. For instance, a series of wash trades that generate substantial volume can make it appear as though there is strong interest in buying Bitcoin, leading other traders to follow suit and push the price higher. Once the price has been driven up, the manipulators can then sell their holdings at a profit, leaving other investors to suffer the subsequent price decline when the artificial demand dissipates.

The impact of wash trading extends beyond individual losses. It undermines the integrity of the Bitcoin market by distorting the natural supply and demand dynamics, making it difficult for traders to make informed decisions based on genuine market conditions. This distortion can lead to increased volatility, as price movements driven by false trading activity are more likely to result in sharp corrections once the manipulation is uncovered. Moreover, the prevalence of wash trading can erode trust in the market, deterring new investors and stifling the growth of the Bitcoin ecosystem.

The lack of stringent regulatory oversight in the Bitcoin market has allowed wash trading to proliferate. Unlike traditional financial markets, which are subject to regulatory scrutiny and enforcement, the cryptocurrency market operates with minimal regulation. This regulatory gap creates an environment where manipulators can engage in wash trading with little fear of repercussions. Efforts to combat wash trading in the Bitcoin market have been limited, partly due to the pseudonymous nature of transactions and the global, decentralized structure of the market.

Addressing wash trading requires a multifaceted approach. Increased regulatory oversight and enforcement are crucial for deterring manipulators and protecting investors. Regulatory bodies can implement and enforce rules that prohibit wash trading and impose penalties on those who engage in such practices. Exchanges also play a critical role in combating wash trading by implementing robust monitoring and surveillance systems to detect and prevent suspicious trading activity. Transparency and accountability measures, such as requiring exchanges to report accurate trading volumes and disclose trading practices, can further help in curbing wash trading.

Educating investors about the signs of wash trading and the risks associated with manipulated markets is another important step. By raising awareness about these deceptive practices, investors can become more vigilant and better equipped to recognize and avoid manipulation. Additionally, promoting the development and adoption of decentralized exchanges (DEXs) can help reduce the prevalence of wash trading. DEXs operate without central intermediaries, making it more challenging for manipulators to execute coordinated wash trades.

In conclusion, wash trading is a significant challenge in the Bitcoin market, exploiting the unregulated environment and the pseudonymous nature of transactions. This deceptive practice distorts market dynamics, increases volatility, and undermines investor confidence. Addressing wash trading requires a combination of regulatory oversight, exchange vigilance, and investor education. By tackling this issue, the Bitcoin market can move towards greater transparency, integrity, and stability, fostering a healthier and more trustworthy trading environment.

Coordinated Market Manipulation

Coordinated market manipulation is a critical issue in the Bitcoin market, where influential entities, often known as 'whales,' use their significant holdings to orchestrate price movements to their advantage. This form of manipulation involves strategic collaboration among multiple players to create artificial market conditions that mislead other participants, resulting in significant financial gains for the manipulators and losses for unsuspecting investors.

The mechanics of coordinated market manipulation are sophisticated and deliberate. Whales, who control substantial amounts of Bitcoin, can influence the market by executing large buy or sell orders in a synchronized manner. For example, a group of whales might decide to buy large quantities of Bitcoin within a short timeframe, creating an impression of high demand and driving the price upward. This artificial price inflation can attract additional buyers, including retail investors and algorithmic traders, who interpret the rising prices as a signal of genuine market interest. Once the price has been sufficiently inflated, the whales then sell their holdings at the peak, profiting from the elevated prices while causing the market to crash when the artificial demand disappears.

Another common tactic used in coordinated manipulation is spoofing. Spoofing involves placing large buy or sell orders on the order book with no intention of executing them. These orders create a false impression of supply and demand, influencing the market price. For instance, a manipulator might place a large sell order to drive the price down, only to cancel the order once the price reaches a lower target, allowing them to buy at a cheaper rate. Similarly, placing large buy orders can drive the price up, allowing the manipulator to sell at higher prices. Spoofing distorts the natural price discovery process and creates volatility, making it challenging for traders to make informed decisions based on true market conditions.

Pump and dump schemes are another manifestation of coordinated market manipulation. In these schemes, the price of Bitcoin is artificially inflated through misleading information and hype, usually propagated through social media, forums, and private chat groups. The orchestrators of the scheme buy Bitcoin at lower prices and then 'pump' the price by creating a buying frenzy. Once the price has been driven to a desired level, they 'dump' their holdings, selling off their Bitcoin at the inflated prices and causing the market to crash. Retail investors who bought in during the pump phase are left with significant losses when the price collapses.

The impact of coordinated market manipulation extends beyond individual financial losses. It undermines the integrity of the Bitcoin market, leading to mistrust among investors and reducing overall market participation. When prices are manipulated, the natural supply and demand dynamics are distorted, making it difficult for traders to rely on market signals for decision-making. This manipulation contributes to the extreme volatility observed in the Bitcoin market, which can deter institutional investors and stifle the adoption of Bitcoin as a stable financial asset.

Addressing coordinated market manipulation requires a multifaceted approach involving regulatory oversight, market surveillance, and increased transparency. Regulatory bodies need to implement stringent rules against manipulative practices and enforce penalties for violations. Exchanges play a crucial role in detecting and preventing manipulation by monitoring trading patterns and implementing robust surveillance systems. Transparency measures, such as requiring exchanges to report accurate trading volumes and disclose significant trading activities, can help in identifying and curbing manipulation.

Educating investors about the risks and signs of market manipulation is also essential. By raising awareness of these practices, investors can become more vigilant and better equipped to protect themselves from manipulative schemes. Encouraging the use of decentralized exchanges (DEXs), which operate without central intermediaries, can reduce the prevalence of coordinated manipulation, as these platforms make it more challenging for manipulators to coordinate large-scale activities.

In conclusion, coordinated market manipulation is a pervasive issue in the Bitcoin market, driven by the actions of powerful entities who exploit their significant holdings to influence prices. This manipulation undermines market integrity, distorts price discovery, and erodes investor confidence. Combating these practices requires comprehensive regulatory measures, effective market surveillance, and increased transparency. By addressing the root causes of manipulation and promoting ethical trading practices, the Bitcoin market can move towards greater stability and trustworthiness, fostering a healthier environment for all participants.

Impact of Speculation

Role of Speculators

Speculators play a crucial role in the Bitcoin market, driving both its volatility and liquidity. These market participants engage in buying and selling Bitcoin primarily for short-term profit rather than long-term investment. Their actions are driven by the anticipation of price movements, often based on market sentiment, technical analysis, or news events. Speculators contribute to the dynamic nature of the Bitcoin market, creating opportunities and risks for other traders and investors.

The presence of speculators in the Bitcoin market is a double-edged sword. On one hand, they provide much-needed liquidity, enabling other participants to buy or sell Bitcoin with relative ease. This liquidity is essential for the functioning of the market, as it ensures that there are always buyers and sellers available, facilitating smoother and more efficient transactions. Higher liquidity generally leads to narrower bid-ask spreads, reducing transaction costs and making the market more attractive to participants.

On the other hand, the speculative nature of their trading can lead to increased volatility. Speculators often react quickly to news, rumors, and market trends, which can result in significant price swings. For example, a positive news event such as the announcement of a major company accepting Bitcoin as payment can trigger a buying frenzy among speculators, driving the price up rapidly. Conversely, negative news such as regulatory crackdowns can lead to panic selling, causing sharp declines in price. These rapid and often exaggerated price movements can create an unpredictable trading environment, making it challenging for other market participants to navigate.

The strategies employed by speculators vary widely, ranging from day trading to swing trading, and often involve the use of leverage to amplify potential gains. Day traders buy and sell Bitcoin within the same trading day, capitalizing on short-term price fluctuations. Swing traders, on the other hand, hold positions for several days or weeks, aiming to profit from medium-term price trends. Both strategies rely heavily on technical analysis, which involves analyzing historical price data and chart patterns to predict future price movements. While these strategies can be highly profitable, they also carry significant risks, particularly when leverage is involved, as it can magnify both gains and losses.

Speculators also play a role in the phenomenon of market bubbles and crashes. During a bull market, the optimistic sentiment and FOMO (fear of missing out) can drive speculative buying, pushing prices to unsustainable levels. This speculative fervor can create a bubble, where prices are driven more by market sentiment and speculation than by underlying fundamentals. When the bubble bursts, often triggered by a shift in sentiment or negative news, the resulting sell-off can lead to a market crash, with prices plummeting rapidly. These boom-and-bust cycles are a characteristic feature of the Bitcoin market, largely driven by speculative activity.

Despite the risks and volatility associated with speculation, it also has positive aspects. Speculative trading contributes to the discovery of Bitcoin's price, as the collective actions of speculators and other market participants reflect their perceptions of Bitcoin's value. This price discovery process is essential for the market to function efficiently, as it ensures that Bitcoin's price adjusts to reflect new information and changing market conditions. Additionally, the presence of speculators can attract more participants to the market, increasing its overall size and depth.

Moreover, speculators can provide a counterbalance to other market forces. For example, if a large sell-off occurs due to panic selling, speculators might step in to buy Bitcoin at lower prices, providing support and helping to stabilize the market. Similarly, during periods of excessive optimism, speculators might sell Bitcoin to lock in profits, preventing the market from overheating. In this way, speculative trading can contribute to the overall stability and resilience of the market, despite its short-term impact on volatility.

In conclusion, speculators play a vital role in the Bitcoin market, contributing to its liquidity, volatility, and price discovery. While their actions can lead to significant price swings and market instability, they also provide essential liquidity and help to ensure that Bitcoin's price reflects current market conditions. Understanding the role of speculators and their impact on the market is crucial for anyone looking to navigate the complex and dynamic world of Bitcoin trading. By recognizing the influence of speculative activity, traders and investors can better anticipate market movements and make more informed decisions.

Behavioral Economics

Behavioral economics offers a valuable lens through which to examine the Bitcoin market, providing insights into how psychological factors and cognitive biases influence the behavior of market participants. Traditional economic theories often assume that individuals act rationally to maximize their utility, but behavioral economics acknowledges that human behavior is often irrational and influenced by a variety of psychological factors. This understanding is crucial for analyzing the volatility and price movements of Bitcoin.

One of the most relevant concepts in behavioral economics is the role of heuristics, which are mental shortcuts that people use to make decisions quickly. While heuristics can be useful, they often lead to biases that can skew decision-making. In the context of Bitcoin, one common heuristic is the availability bias, where investors make decisions based on recent events or readily available information rather than a comprehensive analysis. For example, if the price of Bitcoin has recently surged, investors might assume that it will continue to rise and rush to buy more, contributing to speculative bubbles.

Another important concept is the prospect theory, which describes how people value gains and losses differently. According to this theory, individuals are more sensitive to losses than to gains of the same magnitude, a phenomenon known as loss aversion. In the Bitcoin market, this can lead to panic selling when prices start to drop, as investors rush to avoid further losses. This behavior can amplify downward price movements, leading to sharp corrections.

Herd behavior is another significant aspect of behavioral economics that is particularly relevant to Bitcoin. Herd behavior occurs when individuals mimic the actions of a larger group, often ignoring their own analysis or the underlying fundamentals. This behavior is driven by the belief that the majority cannot be wrong, leading to bandwagon effects. In the Bitcoin market, herd behavior can be observed during both bull and bear markets.

During a bull market, the fear of missing out (FOMO) can drive investors to buy Bitcoin as they see others profiting, pushing prices even higher. Conversely, during a bear market, the fear, uncertainty, and doubt (FUD) can lead to widespread selling as investors follow the actions of others, exacerbating price declines.

The concept of overconfidence bias also plays a significant role in the behavior of Bitcoin investors. Overconfidence bias occurs when individuals overestimate their knowledge, abilities, or the precision of their information. In the Bitcoin market, overconfidence can lead to excessive risk-taking and speculative trading. Investors might believe they have superior information or insights about future price movements, prompting them to make larger bets than they otherwise would. This overconfidence can contribute to greater volatility as speculative trades influence market dynamics.

Anchoring is another cognitive bias that affects decision-making in the Bitcoin market. Anchoring occurs when individuals rely too heavily on the first piece of information they receive (the "anchor") when making decisions. For example, if an investor learns that Bitcoin was priced at $60,000 at its peak, they might use this figure as a reference point, expecting prices to return to or exceed this level. This bias can influence their buying and selling decisions, even if current market conditions do not support such price levels.

The disposition effect is a behavioral phenomenon where investors are reluctant to sell assets that have decreased in value but are eager to sell assets that have increased in value. In the Bitcoin market, this effect can lead to irrational holding of losing positions in the hope that prices will rebound, while quickly cashing in on gains to lock in profits. This behavior can distort market dynamics, as it can delay price corrections and create artificial price floors or ceilings.

Behavioral economics also sheds light on the impact of social media and information cascades in the Bitcoin market.

Information cascades occur when individuals make decisions based on the observations or actions of others rather than their own information. Social media platforms like Twitter and Reddit play a significant role in disseminating information (and misinformation) about Bitcoin, often leading to rapid and widespread changes in market sentiment. Positive or negative news can spread quickly, prompting waves of buying or selling that significantly impact prices.

In conclusion, behavioral economics provides a framework for understanding the complex and often irrational behavior of Bitcoin investors. By examining cognitive biases, heuristics, and social influences, we can gain deeper insights into the factors driving Bitcoin's price volatility and market dynamics. Recognizing these behavioral patterns can help investors make more informed decisions and navigate the challenges of the Bitcoin market more effectively. Understanding that human behavior often deviates from rationality is key to comprehending the forces at play in the world of Bitcoin and other cryptocurrencies.

Market Psychology

Market psychology plays a critical role in the behavior of Bitcoin prices, significantly influencing the actions of investors and traders. Unlike traditional financial markets, where fundamentals and economic indicators often drive decisions, the Bitcoin market is heavily swayed by psychological factors. Understanding these factors is essential for navigating the volatile and often unpredictable nature of Bitcoin trading.

Fear and greed are two powerful emotions that dominate market psychology. Greed drives investors to buy Bitcoin in the hope of making quick profits, especially during bull markets when prices are rising rapidly. This emotion is often amplified by the fear of missing out (FOMO), where investors rush to buy Bitcoin to avoid being left out of potential gains. FOMO can lead to irrational buying sprees, pushing prices to unsustainable levels and creating speculative bubbles. During such times, the positive sentiment and herd behavior cause a self-reinforcing cycle of rising prices, attracting even more buyers.

Conversely, fear can trigger mass selling and panic during market downturns. When prices begin to fall, the fear of further losses can lead to widespread panic selling, exacerbating the price decline. This phenomenon is often referred to as FUD—fear, uncertainty, and doubt. Negative news, regulatory crackdowns, or significant market corrections can instill fear among investors, prompting them to sell their holdings to avoid further losses. This behavior can lead to sharp and sudden price drops, creating a highly volatile trading environment.

The impact of cognitive biases on market psychology is profound. Confirmation bias, for example, leads investors to seek out information that supports their existing beliefs while ignoring contrary evidence. In the context of Bitcoin, an investor who believes in the long-term success of Bitcoin may focus only on positive news and ignore signs of market instability or overvaluation. This bias can result in holding onto positions for too long or buying more during market peaks, increasing the risk of significant losses.

Overconfidence bias is another psychological factor that affects market participants. Many investors believe they have superior knowledge or insight into market movements, leading them to take excessive risks. Overconfident investors might underestimate the volatility of Bitcoin or overestimate their ability to predict market trends, resulting in larger-than-expected losses when the market moves against them. This bias is particularly prevalent in the Bitcoin market, where the allure of high returns attracts both seasoned traders and novices.

The anchoring effect also plays a significant role in shaping investor decisions. This bias occurs when individuals rely too heavily on an initial piece of information (the "anchor") when making decisions. For example, if an investor buys Bitcoin at a high price, they may anchor their expectations to that price level and be reluctant to sell at a lower price, even if market conditions suggest further declines. This can lead to irrational holding patterns and increased susceptibility to losses during bear markets.

Market sentiment is heavily influenced by external factors such as news, social media, and influential personalities. Positive or negative news can quickly spread through social media platforms, significantly impacting market sentiment and driving price movements. For instance, an endorsement from a prominent figure or positive regulatory news can boost investor confidence and drive up prices. Conversely, negative news such as hacks, regulatory crackdowns, or critical statements from influential figures can lead to panic selling and sharp price declines.

The role of social proof in market psychology cannot be understated. Social proof is the tendency of individuals to follow the actions of others, believing that those actions reflect the correct behavior. In the Bitcoin market, this often manifests in herd behavior, where investors follow the majority without conducting their own analysis. When influential investors or a significant portion of the market starts buying or selling, others tend to follow suit, amplifying price movements and volatility.

Understanding market psychology is crucial for developing effective trading strategies. Successful traders and investors often adopt a contrarian approach, going against the prevailing market sentiment. When the market is overly optimistic, contrarian investors may sell or reduce their positions, anticipating a correction. Conversely, when the market is driven by fear and prices are falling, they may buy, expecting a rebound once the panic subsides. This approach requires discipline and a deep understanding of market psychology, as well as the ability to manage emotions and biases.

Risk management is another essential aspect of navigating market psychology. Setting stop-loss orders, diversifying investments, and maintaining a long-term perspective can help mitigate the impact of emotional decision-making. By having a well-defined risk management strategy, investors can reduce the likelihood of making impulsive decisions driven by fear or greed.

In conclusion, market psychology plays a pivotal role in the behavior of Bitcoin prices. Fear, greed, cognitive biases, and social influences all contribute to the volatility and unpredictability of the Bitcoin market. By understanding these psychological factors, investors can better navigate the complexities of Bitcoin trading, make more informed decisions, and develop strategies to manage risk effectively. Recognizing the impact of market psychology is crucial for achieving long-term success in the dynamic and often turbulent world of Bitcoin.

Chapter 3: The Whales: Who They Are and What They Do

Identifying the Whales

Definition of a Whale

A whale in the context of Bitcoin and cryptocurrency markets refers to an individual or entity that holds a significant amount of Bitcoin, enough to influence market prices with their trading actions. These large holders can be early adopters, institutional investors, hedge funds, or even cryptocurrency exchanges that control substantial amounts of Bitcoin. The term "whale" is used because, much like the largest creatures in the ocean, these market participants have the power to create large waves and impact the environment around them.

Whales play a pivotal role in the cryptocurrency ecosystem. Due to their significant holdings, their buying or selling actions can lead to substantial price movements. When a whale decides to buy a large quantity of Bitcoin, it can create upward pressure on the price, as the increased demand pushes prices higher. Conversely, when a whale sells a large amount of Bitcoin, it can create downward pressure, leading to price drops as the market absorbs the increased supply.

The presence of whales can lead to market manipulation, intentionally or unintentionally. When whales make large trades, they can cause sudden and dramatic price fluctuations. For instance, a whale selling a significant portion of their holdings can lead to panic among smaller investors, who may then also start selling to avoid losses, exacerbating the price decline. This can create a cascading effect, where the initial action by the whale triggers a broader market reaction.

Moreover, whales can engage in deliberate strategies to manipulate the market for their benefit. One common tactic is the "pump and dump" scheme, where a whale accumulates Bitcoin over time and then creates hype or positive news to drive up the price. Once the price reaches a desirable level, the whale sells off their holdings at the peak, making substantial profits while leaving other investors with significant losses when the price inevitably crashes.

Another strategy involves "spoofing," where a whale places large buy or sell orders to create the illusion of market interest, without intending to execute these orders. This can manipulate the market's perception of supply and demand, influencing other traders to act based on the false signals. Once the desired price movement occurs, the whale cancels their spoof orders and executes trades in the direction they intended to profit from.

The activities of whales can also lead to psychological impacts on the market. The knowledge that a few large holders can significantly influence prices can create uncertainty and fear among smaller investors. This uncertainty can lead to increased volatility, as traders react to the perceived actions of whales rather than to fundamental market conditions. Additionally, the presence of whales can lead to reduced market confidence, as investors may feel that the market is rigged in favor of these large players.

Despite the potential negative impacts, whales also provide essential liquidity to the market. Their large trades can help facilitate transactions and maintain market efficiency. In periods of low trading activity, the presence of whales can ensure that there is enough volume for smaller traders to buy and sell Bitcoin without significant price slippage.

In conclusion, the definition of a whale in the Bitcoin market encompasses any individual or entity with substantial Bitcoin holdings capable of influencing market prices. While whales can provide necessary liquidity, their actions can also lead to significant price volatility and potential market manipulation. Understanding the role of whales is crucial for navigating the complexities of the Bitcoin market and recognizing the potential for both risks and opportunities they present. As the cryptocurrency market continues to evolve, the influence of whales remains a critical factor in shaping market dynamics and investor behavior.

Whale Strategies

Whale strategies in the Bitcoin market are diverse and sophisticated, reflecting the significant influence these large holders have over market dynamics. By understanding these strategies, one can gain insight into the mechanisms behind Bitcoin's price movements and the broader implications for market participants.

One common strategy employed by whales is the deliberate creation of price volatility through large buy and sell orders. This approach takes advantage of the liquidity constraints in the market. For example, a whale might place a series of large buy orders to drive up the price of Bitcoin. This sudden increase in demand can create a buying frenzy among smaller investors, pushing the price even higher. Once the price has reached a desirable peak, the whale then executes large sell orders, capitalizing on the elevated price and triggering a market sell-off. This sell-off can cause panic among smaller investors, leading to a sharp decline in price as they rush to exit their positions. This strategy allows whales to profit from both the rise and fall of Bitcoin prices, exploiting the market's reaction to their trades.

Another sophisticated tactic is wash trading, where a whale simultaneously buys and sells Bitcoin to create an illusion of high trading volume. This practice can mislead other market participants into believing there is significant market activity, potentially attracting more traders and increasing liquidity. The increased volume can also influence the price, as it may be perceived as a signal of strong market interest. By creating false trading volume, whales can manipulate market sentiment and drive prices in their favor.

Pump and dump schemes are another notorious strategy used by whales. In these schemes, a group of coordinated traders artificially inflates the price of Bitcoin by disseminating positive news and hype, often through social media and forums. As the price rises, driven by the influx of new investors caught up in the excitement, the orchestrators of the scheme sell off their holdings at the peak, making substantial profits. The subsequent crash in price leaves latecomers with significant losses. These schemes exploit the fear of missing out (FOMO) and the herd mentality prevalent among retail investors.

Spoofing is another manipulative strategy employed by whales. This involves placing large buy or sell orders without the intention of executing them. These orders are used to create the illusion of market pressure in one direction, prompting other traders to react. For instance, a whale might place a large sell order, signaling a potential price drop. As other traders start selling in response, the whale cancels the spoof order and buys at the now-lower price. This tactic can be used to manipulate prices without actually trading large amounts of Bitcoin, allowing whales to influence market movements subtly and efficiently.

Front running is a strategy where whales exploit their knowledge of upcoming large trades to benefit from the anticipated price movements. For example, if a whale knows that a large buy order is about to be executed, they can buy Bitcoin beforehand, driving the price up. Once the large order is executed and the price rises further, the whale sells their holdings at a profit. This strategy takes advantage of the time lag between order placements and executions, using privileged information to gain an edge over other market participants.

Whales also use arbitrage opportunities across different exchanges to profit from price discrepancies. By buying Bitcoin on one exchange where the price is lower and selling it on another where the price is higher, whales can make risk-free profits. This strategy requires significant capital and quick execution to be effective, often utilizing automated trading algorithms to identify and exploit these opportunities in real time.

Market making is another approach where whales provide liquidity to the market by placing both buy and sell orders around the current price. This strategy helps stabilize prices and reduce volatility, earning whales a profit from the bid-ask spread. By consistently providing liquidity, whales can influence the market dynamics and maintain a degree of control over price movements.

In conclusion, whale strategies in the Bitcoin market are varied and complex, leveraging large capital and sophisticated tactics to manipulate prices and profit from market movements. These strategies include creating artificial volatility, wash trading, pump and dump schemes, spoofing, front running, arbitrage, and market making. Understanding these strategies is crucial for recognizing the signs of manipulation and making informed decisions in the Bitcoin market. The influence of whales underscores the importance of regulatory measures and market surveillance to ensure a fair and transparent trading environment for all participants.

Whales vs. Retail Investors

Whales and retail investors are two distinct groups within the Bitcoin market, each with different levels of influence, resources, and strategies. The interactions between these groups often shape the overall market dynamics, creating a complex and sometimes contentious environment.

Whales are individuals or entities that hold large quantities of Bitcoin. Due to their substantial holdings, whales have the power to influence Bitcoin prices through their trading activities. They can execute large buy or sell orders, causing significant price movements that can trigger broader market reactions. For example, when a whale decides to sell a large amount of Bitcoin, it can lead to a sharp decline in prices, causing panic among smaller investors who might start selling their holdings to avoid further losses. This cascading effect can exacerbate price drops, highlighting the outsized influence that whales wield in the market.

In contrast, retail investors are individual traders or small-scale investors who buy and sell Bitcoin in smaller quantities. Retail investors often lack the resources and market influence that whales possess. Their trading decisions are typically based on market trends, news, and technical analysis, rather than the ability to manipulate prices. Despite their smaller individual impact, retail investors collectively contribute to the market's liquidity and can influence price movements through collective behavior.

One of the key differences between whales and retail investors is their trading strategies. Whales often use sophisticated strategies, including market manipulation tactics, to maximize their profits. They might engage in practices such as spoofing, where they place large buy or sell orders without the intention of executing them, to create false market signals and manipulate prices. Another common strategy is wash trading, where a whale simultaneously buys and sells Bitcoin to create the illusion of high trading volume and influence market sentiment.

Retail investors, on the other hand, typically lack the capacity to engage in such manipulative tactics. Their strategies are often based on fundamental or technical analysis, and they rely on market signals and news to inform their trading decisions. Retail investors are more susceptible to the influence of whales and other market forces, and their actions are often reactive rather than proactive. For example, retail investors might buy Bitcoin during a price surge driven by whale activity, only to suffer losses when the whales sell off their holdings and the price drops.

The relationship between whales and retail investors is inherently imbalanced, with whales having a significant advantage due to their financial resources and market influence. This imbalance can lead to market manipulation, where whales exploit their position to profit at the expense of retail investors. The actions of whales can create volatile market conditions, making it challenging for retail investors to navigate the market and protect their investments.

Despite these challenges, the presence of retail investors is crucial for the Bitcoin market. They provide liquidity, enabling more efficient price discovery and smoother market operations. Retail investors also contribute to the decentralized nature of the Bitcoin ecosystem, helping to distribute Bitcoin ownership more broadly. However, the impact of their collective behavior, often driven by fear and greed, can amplify market volatility. For instance, during periods of rapid price increases, retail investors driven by FOMO may push prices even higher, creating speculative bubbles. Conversely, during market downturns, panic selling among retail investors can accelerate price declines.

To mitigate the impact of whale activity and protect retail investors, regulatory measures and market transparency are essential. Regulatory oversight can help prevent manipulative practices such as spoofing and wash trading, fostering a fairer trading environment. Exchanges can also play a role by implementing stricter monitoring and surveillance to detect and prevent manipulation. Additionally, educating retail investors about the risks and signs of market manipulation can empower them to make more informed decisions and avoid falling victim to manipulative tactics.

In conclusion, the dynamics between whales and retail investors are a defining feature of the Bitcoin market. While whales have the power to influence prices and engage in sophisticated trading strategies, retail investors provide essential liquidity and contribute to the decentralized ethos of Bitcoin. Understanding the interactions between these groups is crucial for navigating the Bitcoin market and recognizing the potential for manipulation. By promoting transparency, regulation, and investor education, the market can move towards a more equitable and stable trading environment.

Whale Activities and Market Impact

Case Studies of Whale Movements

Case studies of whale movements provide valuable insights into how these large holders can influence Bitcoin's market dynamics, often leading to significant price fluctuations. These case studies highlight the strategies employed by whales and the broader implications for retail investors and the market as a whole.

One notable example occurred in late 2017, during Bitcoin's historic bull run. As Bitcoin approached its all-time high near $20,000, several large transactions were observed on the blockchain, suggesting that whales were moving substantial amounts of Bitcoin between wallets. These movements often preceded significant price increases, indicating that whales were accumulating Bitcoin in anticipation of higher prices. As retail investors joined the fray, driven by FOMO and the widespread media coverage, the price surged even further. However, as the price peaked, many of these whales began to sell off their holdings. The subsequent sell-off led to a sharp decline in prices, triggering panic among retail investors and resulting in a rapid market crash. This sequence of accumulation, distribution, and sell-off exemplifies how whale movements can create and burst speculative bubbles.

Another significant case study involves the activities of whales during the market correction in early 2021. After Bitcoin reached a new all-time high of approximately $64,000 in April, a series of large sell orders were placed on various exchanges. Blockchain analysis revealed that these sell orders were likely initiated by a few large holders who had amassed Bitcoin at lower prices. The massive sell-off led to a dramatic price drop, with Bitcoin losing nearly 50% of its value within a few weeks. This market correction highlighted the influence of whale sell-offs in creating downward pressure on prices and exacerbating market volatility. Retail investors who bought Bitcoin during the peak experienced significant losses, underscoring the risks associated with following market trends driven by whale activities.

A different aspect of whale behavior was observed during the market recovery in mid-2021. As Bitcoin's price began to stabilize around $30,000, several large buy orders were placed, indicating that whales were re-entering the market. These buy orders provided liquidity and helped stabilize prices, creating a floor that prevented further declines. The presence of whale buying activity signaled to retail investors that the market might be poised for recovery, leading to increased buying interest and a subsequent price rebound. This case study illustrates how whale buying can provide support during market downturns, contributing to market stability and recovery.

The infamous Mt. Gox incident offers another instructive case study. Mt. Gox was once the largest Bitcoin exchange, handling over 70% of all Bitcoin transactions worldwide. In 2014, it collapsed after losing approximately 850,000 Bitcoins, many of which belonged to its users. The subsequent legal proceedings revealed that a single entity, dubbed "Tokyo Whale," was responsible for selling large amounts of Bitcoin recovered from the exchange's bankruptcy. These sales were conducted in a manner that significantly impacted market prices, leading to substantial volatility. The Tokyo Whale's actions highlight how the liquidation of large Bitcoin holdings, whether by an individual or an institution, can lead to market instability and affect the broader ecosystem.

One of the most recent examples of whale influence occurred in late 2023, when a coordinated effort by several large holders led to a significant market rally. These whales began accumulating Bitcoin quietly over several months, using various wallets to avoid detection. Once their positions were established, they coordinated their buying to drive the price up sharply over a short period. This sudden price increase attracted media attention and retail investors, who rushed to buy in, further amplifying the price rise. The whales then began to sell their holdings in stages, realizing significant profits while the market experienced heightened volatility. This coordinated effort underscores the power of whales to manipulate market sentiment and create artificial price movements.

These case studies demonstrate the profound impact that whale movements can have on the Bitcoin market. By leveraging their substantial holdings, whales can create significant price swings, influence market sentiment, and generate volatility that can be both profitable for them and challenging for retail investors. Understanding these dynamics is crucial for anyone participating in the Bitcoin market, as it highlights the importance of recognizing the signs of whale activity and the potential implications for price movements. The influence of whales underscores the need for greater market transparency and regulatory oversight to mitigate the risks of manipulation and ensure a fairer trading environment for all participants.

Large Transactions and Price Swings

Large transactions and their impact on Bitcoin price swings have become a focal point in understanding market dynamics. When whales, or large Bitcoin holders, make significant trades, the market often reacts sharply. These reactions stem from the sheer volume of Bitcoins involved, which can create substantial shifts in supply and demand.

One illustrative case occurred in 2020 when a series of large transactions led to notable price movements. A whale transferred 88,857 Bitcoins, valued at over $1 billion at the time, to various exchanges. The news of this transfer caused market anxiety, leading many retail investors to anticipate a major sell-off. As a result, Bitcoin's price dropped nearly 10% within hours. This incident underscores how large transactions can create panic and drive market sentiment, even before the actual selling begins.

Another example took place in early 2021. A whale deposited 28,000 Bitcoins into Coinbase, a major exchange, fueling speculation of an impending sale. Although the whale did not immediately sell the Bitcoins, the deposit alone was enough to trigger a significant price decline. This preemptive market reaction highlights the psychological impact of large transactions. Investors often assume that such deposits will be followed by selling, prompting them to sell their own holdings to avoid potential losses, thus driving the price down.

Moreover, the influence of large transactions is not limited to direct price impacts. They can also affect liquidity, a crucial factor in price stability. When a whale conducts a large buy order, it can quickly absorb available sell orders, leading to a temporary liquidity crunch. This reduction in available Bitcoins can cause prices to spike as other buyers compete for the remaining supply. Conversely, a large sell order can flood the market with Bitcoins, overwhelming buy orders and driving the price down sharply. These liquidity effects can create short-term volatility, exacerbating the already unpredictable nature of the Bitcoin market.

The significance of these large transactions extends beyond immediate price swings. They also influence market perception and sentiment. For instance, when large holders move Bitcoins to exchanges, it often generates headlines and social media buzz. This increased visibility can amplify market reactions, as more traders become aware of the potential for significant price movements. In this way, the actions of whales not only impact the market through their trades but also through the broader narrative they create.

One notable instance is the 2017 bull run, which saw Bitcoin's price rise from $1,000 to nearly $20,000 within a year. During this period, several large transactions were executed by whales, including both buys and sells. These transactions were often coordinated to capitalize on market momentum, with whales buying during dips and selling during peaks. This strategic trading amplified the overall price movement, contributing to the rapid rise and subsequent crash. The coordinated nature of these trades underscores the power of large holders to shape market trends and influence the broader investment community.

In addition to immediate price and liquidity impacts, large transactions can have longer-term effects on market structure. For example, sustained large buys can create higher support levels, as the market adjusts to the increased demand. Conversely, continuous large sells can establish lower resistance levels, making it harder for prices to rebound. These structural changes can persist, influencing market behavior long after the initial transactions.

Another critical aspect is the role of blockchain transparency in tracking these large transactions. The public ledger allows anyone to observe significant movements of Bitcoin, providing insights into whale activity. This transparency can be a double-edged sword. On one hand, it promotes market integrity by allowing all participants to see major trades. On the other hand, it can also contribute to volatility, as traders react to observed movements, often leading to speculative behavior.

The implications of large transactions are further complicated by the strategies employed by whales. Techniques such as wash trading, where a trader buys and sells the same asset to create artificial trading volume, can distort market perceptions. Similarly, spoofing, where a trader places large orders with no intention of executing them, can mislead other participants about market conditions. These manipulative practices can exacerbate the impact of large transactions, creating misleading signals that drive volatility.

In conclusion, large transactions by whales play a pivotal role in Bitcoin's market dynamics, influencing prices, liquidity, and overall sentiment. Their actions can create immediate and significant price swings, alter market structure, and drive long-term trends. Understanding these impacts is crucial for navigating the complexities of the Bitcoin market, highlighting the need for greater market transparency and robust regulatory oversight to mitigate the risks associated with such large-scale trading activities.

The Ripple Effect

The ripple effect in the Bitcoin market refers to the cascading impact that significant events or actions by major market participants, such as whales, can have on the broader market. This phenomenon can be observed through various mechanisms, including large transactions, market sentiment shifts, and regulatory announcements, all of which can trigger a chain reaction affecting prices, trading volumes, and investor behavior.

One notable instance of the ripple effect occurred when a whale moved a substantial amount of Bitcoin into an exchange wallet. Such a move typically signals a potential sell-off, causing immediate concern among market participants. As news of the transaction spread, other investors began to panic, leading to widespread selling and a sharp decline in Bitcoin's price. This initial action by the whale did not just impact the immediate price but also led to increased volatility as other traders reacted to the falling prices, further amplifying the downward trend.

Another aspect of the ripple effect is the influence of market sentiment. When a prominent figure in the cryptocurrency space makes a public statement about Bitcoin, it can have far-reaching implications. For example, positive comments from influential investors can boost market confidence, leading to a buying spree and significant price increases. Conversely, negative remarks or predictions of regulatory crackdowns can instill fear, prompting mass sell-offs. These sentiment-driven movements often start with a small group of informed traders but quickly spread throughout the market, creating broader price swings.

The introduction of new regulations or changes in regulatory stance also exemplifies the ripple effect. For instance, when a major country announces tighter regulations on cryptocurrency trading, the immediate reaction might be a localized market downturn. However, as the news disseminates globally, it can lead to a widespread loss of confidence in Bitcoin, triggering a global sell-off. The interconnected nature of cryptocurrency markets means that regulatory changes in one region can have a profound impact worldwide, demonstrating the far-reaching consequences of such announcements.

The ripple effect is not limited to negative outcomes. Positive developments, such as the adoption of Bitcoin by major financial institutions or countries, can trigger a wave of optimism. When a country like El Salvador declared Bitcoin as legal tender, it not only boosted Bitcoin's price but also led to increased interest and investment in other cryptocurrencies. This move prompted other nations to consider similar actions, creating a domino effect that bolstered market sentiment and led to a period of bullish activity.

Market manipulation tactics employed by whales can also create ripple effects. For example, a coordinated pump and dump scheme might begin with a group of whales artificially inflating the price of Bitcoin by buying large quantities within a short period. This sudden price increase attracts attention, leading retail investors to jump in, further driving up the price. Once the price reaches a peak, the whales sell off their holdings, causing the price to plummet. The initial manipulation by the whales thus triggers a chain reaction of buying and selling among retail investors, amplifying the price volatility.

Moreover, technological advancements and integrations can induce ripple effects in the market. The launch of Bitcoin futures trading on major exchanges like the Chicago Mercantile Exchange (CME) in 2017 is a prime example. The introduction of futures trading provided institutional investors with new tools for hedging and speculation, leading to increased trading volumes and greater price stability over time. However, it also introduced new dynamics, as futures trading can sometimes decouple from the spot market, leading to complex price movements influenced by both markets.

The interconnectedness of global financial markets means that significant economic events can also trigger ripple effects in the Bitcoin market. For instance, macroeconomic factors such as changes in interest rates, inflation data, or geopolitical tensions can lead to shifts in investor behavior across various asset classes, including Bitcoin. During times of economic uncertainty, Bitcoin is often viewed as a hedge against traditional financial markets, leading to increased buying and price appreciation.

Conversely, when confidence in traditional markets is high, Bitcoin might see decreased interest and price declines.

In conclusion, the ripple effect in the Bitcoin market illustrates the complex interplay between various factors and their far-reaching consequences. Large transactions, market sentiment shifts, regulatory changes, and technological advancements all contribute to this phenomenon. Understanding the ripple effect is crucial for investors and traders, as it highlights the importance of considering broader market dynamics and potential chain reactions when making investment decisions. By recognizing the interconnected nature of these factors, market participants can better navigate the volatility and opportunities within the Bitcoin market.

The Ethics and Legality of Whale Behavior

Ethical Considerations

Ethical considerations in the Bitcoin market are multifaceted and involve a range of issues from market manipulation to the implications of decentralization. As Bitcoin and other cryptocurrencies gain prominence, the ethical landscape surrounding their use and regulation becomes increasingly complex.

One of the primary ethical concerns in the Bitcoin market is market manipulation. Whales, or large holders of Bitcoin, have the power to influence market prices significantly through their trading activities. These actions can create artificial price movements, which can mislead other investors and cause significant financial harm. For example, when whales engage in practices like pump and dump schemes, they inflate the price of Bitcoin through coordinated buying, attract other investors, and then sell off their holdings at the peak, leaving smaller investors with substantial losses. Such manipulative tactics undermine the principles of a fair and transparent market, eroding trust among participants.

The decentralized nature of Bitcoin, while one of its core strengths, also presents ethical challenges. Unlike traditional financial systems that have centralized regulatory bodies to oversee activities and protect investors, the Bitcoin market operates without a central authority. This decentralization means that there is no single entity responsible for monitoring and preventing unethical practices. As a result, investors are more vulnerable to fraudulent schemes and market manipulation. The lack of regulation can also lead to the proliferation of scams, such as initial coin offering (ICO) frauds, where investors are promised high returns on new cryptocurrencies that often turn out to be worthless.

Another ethical issue is the environmental impact of Bitcoin mining. Bitcoin relies on a proof-of-work mechanism, which requires substantial computational power to validate transactions and create new blocks on the blockchain. This process consumes a significant amount of electricity, often sourced from non-renewable energy, contributing to carbon emissions and environmental degradation. The ethical dilemma arises from balancing the benefits of a decentralized financial system against the environmental costs associated with maintaining the network. As the world becomes more conscious of environmental issues, the sustainability of Bitcoin's energy consumption continues to be a contentious topic.

Privacy and anonymity, while valued by many Bitcoin users, also present ethical dilemmas. Bitcoin transactions are pseudonymous, meaning that while transactions are recorded on the blockchain, the identities of the parties involved are not directly tied to the transactions. This feature can be exploited for illicit activities, such as money laundering, tax evasion, and financing illegal operations. The ethical challenge lies in addressing these illegal activities without undermining the privacy rights of legitimate users. Striking a balance between protecting user privacy and ensuring compliance with legal and regulatory standards is a critical issue for the cryptocurrency community.

The potential for wealth concentration in the hands of a few is another ethical concern. While Bitcoin was envisioned as a democratizing force in finance, providing equal opportunities for all, the reality is that a significant portion of Bitcoin is controlled by a small number of addresses. This concentration of wealth can lead to economic inequalities and contradicts the egalitarian ideals that underpin the cryptocurrency movement. The influence of these large holders can also lead to power imbalances, where a few individuals or entities can dictate market trends and outcomes, further marginalizing smaller investors.

Furthermore, the speculative nature of the Bitcoin market raises ethical questions about the promotion of Bitcoin as an investment. The high volatility and risk associated with Bitcoin can lead to significant financial losses for inexperienced investors. The ethical issue here involves the responsibility of influencers, promoters, and financial advisors in presenting Bitcoin as a viable investment option. There is a fine line between promoting financial innovation and engaging in misleading or overly optimistic portrayals that can misguide investors.

Regulatory frameworks and their implementation also come with ethical considerations. While regulation is essential to protect investors and maintain market integrity, overly stringent regulations can stifle innovation and limit the potential benefits of decentralized technologies. Finding the right balance between regulation and innovation is crucial. Ethical regulatory practices should aim to protect investors without curtailing the fundamental freedoms that Bitcoin and other cryptocurrencies offer.

In conclusion, the ethical considerations surrounding Bitcoin are complex and multifaceted, encompassing issues of market manipulation, environmental impact, privacy, wealth concentration, speculative risks, and regulatory challenges. As Bitcoin continues to evolve and integrate into the global financial system, addressing these ethical issues will be essential for fostering a fair, transparent, and sustainable cryptocurrency ecosystem. By acknowledging and addressing these challenges, the Bitcoin community can work towards realizing the original vision of a decentralized, equitable financial system.

Legal Framework

The legal framework surrounding Bitcoin and other cryptocurrencies is a rapidly evolving landscape, reflecting the challenges and complexities of regulating a decentralized and innovative financial technology. As Bitcoin continues to gain traction globally, different jurisdictions have adopted varying approaches to regulate its use, trading, and integration into the broader financial system.

One of the fundamental legal challenges with Bitcoin is its decentralized nature. Unlike traditional financial instruments that operate within clearly defined regulatory boundaries, Bitcoin operates on a global scale without a central authority. This decentralization complicates the development of a unified regulatory approach. Each country must navigate its own legal, economic, and social contexts to establish regulations that address local concerns while remaining compatible with international standards.

In the United States, Bitcoin is regulated by multiple agencies, each focusing on different aspects of its use. The Securities and Exchange Commission (SEC) regulates Bitcoin as a security when it is used in investment contracts or schemes that qualify under the Howey Test. This test determines whether an asset is a security based on the expectation of profits derived from the efforts of others. As a result, Initial Coin Offerings (ICOs) and certain other cryptocurrency investments fall under SEC jurisdiction. The Commodity Futures Trading Commission (CFTC), on the other hand, classifies Bitcoin as a commodity and regulates its trading in futures and derivatives markets. The Financial Crimes Enforcement Network (FinCEN) oversees Bitcoin transactions to prevent money laundering and other illicit activities, requiring exchanges and certain other businesses to register as Money Services Businesses (MSBs) and comply with Anti-Money Laundering (AML) and Know Your Customer (KYC) regulations.

In the European Union, the regulatory approach to Bitcoin varies among member states, though there is a concerted effort to create a cohesive framework. The Fifth Anti-Money Laundering Directive (5AMLD), which came into effect in January 2020, expanded AML regulations to include cryptocurrency exchanges and wallet providers. This directive requires these entities to implement KYC procedures and report suspicious activities. The proposed Markets in Crypto-Assets Regulation (MiCA) aims to provide a comprehensive regulatory framework for digital assets, covering a wide range of issues from consumer protection to market integrity and financial stability. If adopted, MiCA will standardize regulations across the EU, providing clarity and consistency for market participants.

Asia presents a diverse regulatory environment for Bitcoin. In Japan, Bitcoin is recognized as a legal method of payment under the Payment Services Act. The Financial Services Agency (FSA) oversees cryptocurrency exchanges, requiring them to register and comply with stringent AML and cybersecurity measures. South Korea has also implemented strict regulations, mandating real-name verification for cryptocurrency trading and imposing AML requirements on exchanges. China, however, has taken a more restrictive stance, banning cryptocurrency exchanges and ICOs while still exploring the potential of blockchain technology through government-backed initiatives.

The regulatory landscape in other parts of the world is equally varied. In Australia, Bitcoin is treated as property and subject to capital gains tax. The Australian Transaction Reports and Analysis Centre (AUSTRAC) enforces AML and KYC regulations on cryptocurrency exchanges. In Canada, Bitcoin is regulated as a security when used in investment contracts, and cryptocurrency exchanges must register with the Financial

Transactions and Reports Analysis Centre of Canada (FINTRAC) to comply with AML requirements.

One of the primary regulatory challenges is balancing the need for oversight with the desire to foster innovation. Overly stringent regulations can stifle technological advancements and limit the potential benefits of cryptocurrencies. Conversely, a lack of regulation can lead to market instability, fraud, and other illicit activities. Regulators must strike a balance that protects consumers and maintains market integrity without hindering the growth and adoption of Bitcoin and other cryptocurrencies.

Another significant challenge is the cross-border nature of Bitcoin transactions. Bitcoin operates on a global network, making it difficult for any single jurisdiction to enforce regulations effectively. International cooperation and harmonization of regulatory standards are essential to address issues such as money laundering, terrorist financing, and tax evasion. Organizations like the Financial Action Task Force (FATF) play a crucial role in developing global AML standards and encouraging countries to implement consistent regulations.

The evolving legal framework for Bitcoin also includes the exploration of central bank digital currencies (CBDCs). Many central banks are researching or piloting their own digital currencies as a response to the growing popularity of cryptocurrencies. CBDCs could provide the benefits of digital currencies while maintaining the stability and oversight of traditional financial systems. However, the introduction of CBDCs raises questions about the future role of Bitcoin and other decentralized cryptocurrencies in the financial ecosystem.

In conclusion, the legal framework for Bitcoin is complex and multifaceted, reflecting the challenges of regulating a decentralized and innovative technology. Different jurisdictions have adopted varying approaches to address issues such as market integrity, consumer protection, and financial stability. As Bitcoin continues to evolve, ongoing dialogue and cooperation between regulators, industry participants, and international organizations will be crucial in developing effective and balanced regulations that support innovation while protecting the interests of all stakeholders.

Mitigating Manipulation

Mitigating manipulation in the Bitcoin market is essential to ensuring its stability, transparency, and fairness. As Bitcoin and other cryptocurrencies become more integrated into the global financial system, addressing the issue of market manipulation becomes increasingly urgent. Effective mitigation strategies involve a combination of regulatory measures, technological solutions, and community-driven initiatives.

Regulatory oversight plays a crucial role in mitigating market manipulation. Governments and regulatory bodies around the world are increasingly recognizing the need to develop frameworks that address the unique challenges posed by cryptocurrencies. For instance, regulations that require cryptocurrency exchanges to implement robust Know Your Customer (KYC) and Anti-Money Laundering (AML) procedures can help reduce the anonymity that often facilitates manipulative practices. By ensuring that exchanges maintain high standards of transparency and accountability, regulators can make it more difficult for bad actors to operate within the market.

One example of successful regulatory intervention is the Financial Action Task Force (FATF), which has issued guidelines for the global regulation of cryptocurrencies. These guidelines require exchanges to collect and share information about their customers and transactions, making it easier to track and prevent illicit activities. Compliance with such international standards can significantly reduce the opportunities for market manipulation by increasing the traceability of transactions and the accountability of market participants.

Technological solutions also offer promising avenues for mitigating manipulation. Blockchain technology itself, with its transparent and immutable ledger, provides a foundation for enhancing market integrity. Tools that analyze blockchain data in real-time can detect suspicious activities and potential manipulation, alerting regulators and exchanges to take appropriate action. Advanced analytics and machine learning algorithms can be used to identify patterns indicative of manipulative behavior, such as wash trading, spoofing, and pump and dump schemes.

One innovative approach is the development of decentralized exchanges (DEXs), which operate without a central authority and rely on smart contracts to facilitate trades. DEXs can reduce the risk of manipulation by eliminating the need for intermediaries and enhancing the transparency of transactions. Additionally, the use of oracles and other off-chain data integration mechanisms can provide real-time market data, helping to create a more accurate and reliable trading environment.

Community-driven initiatives are another vital component in the fight against market manipulation. The cryptocurrency community, including developers, traders, and investors, plays a critical role in promoting best practices and ethical behavior. By fostering a culture of transparency and accountability, the community can help identify and expose manipulative activities. Educational efforts aimed at increasing awareness of market manipulation tactics and their impact can empower individual investors to make more informed decisions and recognize red flags.

Transparency initiatives, such as Proof of Reserves audits, can further enhance trust in the market. Exchanges can voluntarily disclose their holdings and transaction data, allowing users to verify that the exchange has sufficient reserves to cover all customer deposits. This level of transparency can deter manipulation by providing a clear and verifiable picture of an exchange's financial health and operational integrity.

Collaboration between regulators, industry participants, and the cryptocurrency community is essential to developing and implementing effective mitigation strategies. Public-private partnerships can facilitate the exchange of information and resources, enabling a more coordinated and comprehensive approach to tackling market manipulation. By working together, stakeholders can develop standardized protocols and best practices that enhance market integrity and protect investors.

International cooperation is also crucial, given the global nature of the cryptocurrency market. Coordinated efforts among regulatory bodies can help address jurisdictional challenges and ensure that manipulative activities are not simply shifted to less regulated markets. Cross-border information sharing and joint enforcement actions can enhance the effectiveness of regulatory measures and create a more level playing field for all market participants.

In conclusion, mitigating manipulation in the Bitcoin market requires a multifaceted approach that combines regulatory oversight, technological innovation, and community engagement. By implementing robust KYC and AML procedures, leveraging blockchain analytics and decentralized technologies, and fostering a culture of transparency and accountability, the cryptocurrency ecosystem can become more resilient to manipulative practices. Collaborative efforts among regulators, industry participants, and the global community are essential to building a fair, transparent, and stable market that fulfills the original promise of Bitcoin as a decentralized and democratized financial system.

Chapter 4: The Tools of Manipulation

Technical Analysis and Its Misuse

Basics of Technical Analysis

Technical analysis is a method used by traders to evaluate and forecast the future price movements of a financial asset based on its historical price and volume data. This approach is particularly popular in the Bitcoin market, where it provides a framework for understanding and predicting the asset's volatile price swings. Unlike fundamental analysis, which considers an asset's intrinsic value based on economic indicators and financial statements, technical analysis focuses on identifying patterns and trends that emerge from market behavior.

At the core of technical analysis are price charts, which visually represent the historical performance of an asset. These charts come in various forms, including line charts, bar charts, and candlestick charts, each offering different levels of detail. Candlestick charts are especially favored in cryptocurrency trading due to their ability to display the opening, closing, high, and low prices within a specific time frame. The visual representation of price movements through candlestick patterns helps traders identify potential reversals and continuation patterns.

One of the fundamental principles of technical analysis is the concept of support and resistance levels. Support levels are price points where an asset tends to find buying interest, preventing the price from falling further. Conversely, resistance levels are price points where selling interest emerges, preventing the price from rising further. These levels are crucial for traders, as they often serve as decision points for entering or exiting trades. When the price breaks through a support or resistance level, it can signal the beginning of a new trend.

Trends are another critical aspect of technical analysis. A trend represents the general direction in which the price of an asset is moving. Trends can be upward (bullish), downward (bearish), or sideways (neutral). Identifying the direction of the trend is essential for traders to align their strategies accordingly. Trend lines, which are drawn on charts to connect significant price points, help in visualizing and confirming the direction of the trend.

Moving averages are commonly used technical indicators that smooth out price data to identify trends over a specific period. The most widely used moving averages are the simple moving average (SMA) and the exponential moving average (EMA). The SMA calculates the average price over a set number of periods, while the EMA gives more weight to recent prices, making it more responsive to new information. Traders often use moving averages to identify trend reversals and generate trading signals when shorter-term moving averages cross above or below longer-term moving averages.

Relative Strength Index (RSI) is another popular technical indicator that measures the speed and change of price movements. RSI is typically used to identify overbought or oversold conditions in the market. An RSI value above 70 suggests that the asset is overbought and may be due for a price correction, while an RSI value below 30 indicates that the asset is oversold and may be due for a price rebound. By monitoring RSI levels, traders can make more informed decisions about when to enter or exit trades.

Volume analysis is also an integral part of technical analysis. Volume refers to the number of units of an asset traded over a specific period. Analyzing volume alongside price movements helps traders understand the strength of a price trend. High trading volume during an upward price movement suggests strong buying interest and confirms the uptrend. Conversely, low volume during a price increase may indicate weak buying interest and a potential reversal.

Chart patterns are formations created by the price movements of an asset, which technical analysts use to predict future price movements. Some common chart patterns include head and shoulders, triangles, and double tops or bottoms. These patterns are categorized as reversal patterns, which signal the end of a trend, or continuation patterns, which indicate that the trend is likely to continue. Recognizing these patterns helps traders anticipate price movements and make strategic trading decisions.

Indicators such as Bollinger Bands, which consist of a moving average and two standard deviation lines, provide additional insights into market volatility and potential price breakouts. When the price moves closer to the upper band, it may indicate that the asset is overbought, while movement towards the lower band suggests that the asset is oversold.

In conclusion, the basics of technical analysis provide traders with a set of tools and methodologies to evaluate and predict Bitcoin's price movements based on historical data. By understanding and applying concepts such as support and resistance levels, trends, moving averages, RSI, volume analysis, and chart patterns, traders can make more informed decisions in the highly volatile Bitcoin market. As Bitcoin continues to evolve and attract more participants, the importance of technical analysis in navigating its complex price dynamics remains paramount.

Manipulative Tactics Using Technical Analysis

Manipulative tactics using technical analysis are sophisticated strategies employed by certain market participants to influence Bitcoin prices for personal gain. These tactics exploit the predictable patterns and signals that technical analysis relies on, deceiving traders and triggering market reactions that the manipulators can profit from.

One common tactic is spoofing, which involves placing large buy or sell orders with no intention of executing them. For instance, a manipulator might place a large buy order to create the illusion of strong demand. This can drive the price up as other traders, interpreting the large order as a bullish signal, start buying in anticipation of a price rise. Once the price has increased, the manipulator cancels the large buy order and sells their holdings at the higher price. The same tactic can be used in reverse with sell orders to drive the price down.

Wash trading is another manipulative practice where a trader simultaneously buys and sells the same asset to create artificial trading volume. This can mislead other market participants into believing that there is significant activity and interest in Bitcoin, potentially driving up the price. The increased volume can also make the market appear more liquid than it actually is, attracting more traders and creating an opportunity for the manipulator to sell at inflated prices. This tactic distorts the true supply and demand dynamics of the market, leading to false price signals.

Pump and dump schemes are perhaps the most notorious form of market manipulation. In these schemes, a group of traders coordinate to buy large quantities of Bitcoin, driving up the price through concerted buying efforts. They simultaneously spread positive news or hype about Bitcoin to attract unsuspecting investors. As the price climbs, more traders buy in, driven by fear of missing out on potential gains. Once the price reaches a peak, the manipulators sell off their holdings en masse, causing the price to crash and leaving the new investors with significant losses. This cycle of artificial inflation and subsequent crash can be highly profitable for the orchestrators but devastating for other market participants.

Market makers, who provide liquidity by placing both buy and sell orders, can also engage in manipulative practices. By setting their buy and sell orders strategically, they can influence the price direction and create the appearance of support or resistance levels. For example, a market maker might place large buy orders at a certain price level to create a floor, encouraging other traders to buy, believing that the price will not fall below that level. Once enough traders have bought in, the market maker can remove their buy orders and let the price fall, profiting from the resulting sell-off.

Another sophisticated tactic is front running, where a trader uses advanced knowledge of upcoming large orders to their advantage. For instance, if a manipulator knows that a large buy order is about to be executed, they can buy Bitcoin beforehand, anticipating that the large order will drive the price up. Once the price increases, they sell their holdings at the higher price. This tactic exploits the time lag between order placement and execution, allowing the manipulator to profit from the predictable market reaction.

Technical analysis tools themselves can be manipulated to create false signals. For instance, moving averages, which smooth out price data to identify trends, can be influenced by large, strategically timed trades. A manipulator might execute a series of trades to drive the price above or below a moving average, triggering buy or sell signals for other traders who rely on these indicators. This can create a self-fulfilling prophecy, where the initial manipulation leads to a broader market reaction that further drives the price in the desired direction.

False breakouts are another tactic used to deceive traders. Manipulators might push the price just above a resistance level or just below a support level, triggering stop-loss orders and automated trading algorithms. This can lead to a surge in buying or selling activity, which the manipulators can then exploit by reversing their positions. The resulting price movement can trap traders who followed the false breakout, causing them to incur losses.

In conclusion, manipulative tactics using technical analysis exploit the predictable nature of trading signals to deceive market participants and create artificial price movements. Tactics such as spoofing, wash trading, pump and dump schemes, strategic market making, front running, and manipulating technical indicators can significantly impact Bitcoin prices. Understanding these tactics and recognizing their signs is crucial for traders to protect themselves and make informed decisions in the highly volatile and often manipulated Bitcoin market.

Impact on Trader Behavior

The behavior of traders in the Bitcoin market is profoundly influenced by the dynamics of technical analysis and the manipulative tactics employed by more influential market participants. Understanding these influences helps in deciphering how trader behavior is shaped and what psychological and strategic adaptations occur in response to market conditions.

Technical analysis is a cornerstone of trading strategies for many Bitcoin traders. It involves studying historical price data and trading volumes to identify patterns and predict future price movements. Traders rely on various technical indicators, such as moving averages, relative strength index (RSI), and Bollinger Bands, to make informed decisions. These tools help traders determine entry and exit points, identify trends, and gauge market momentum. However, the effectiveness of technical analysis can be compromised when manipulative tactics distort the natural market signals.

One of the most significant impacts of manipulation on trader behavior is the amplification of fear and greed. These two emotions are powerful drivers in financial markets, often leading to irrational decision-making. When manipulators employ tactics like spoofing or wash trading, they can create false market signals that exacerbate these emotions. For instance, a sudden, large buy order can trigger a fear of missing out (FOMO) among traders, leading them to buy impulsively and drive the price higher. Conversely, a large sell order can induce panic selling, driven by fear of further losses.

Manipulative practices such as pump and dump schemes also exploit trader psychology. In a pump and dump scenario, the initial artificial price increase lures traders into buying, driven by the belief that the upward trend is genuine and sustainable. Once the price reaches a certain level, the manipulators sell off their holdings, causing the price to plummet. The aftermath often leaves retail traders with significant losses and a deep sense of mistrust towards the market. This cyclical pattern of manipulation can condition traders to be overly cautious or overly aggressive, depending on their previous experiences.

The presence of whales in the market adds another layer of complexity to trader behavior. Whales, with their significant holdings, can move the market substantially. Their actions can either stabilize or destabilize the market, depending on their intentions. When whales accumulate Bitcoin, it can signal to the market that a price increase is forthcoming, leading traders to follow suit and buy. Conversely, when whales start selling, it can lead to a market-wide sell-off. This herd behavior is a direct response to the perceived influence of these large market players.

Technical traders, aware of the potential for manipulation, often develop strategies to mitigate their risks. Some may adopt a more conservative approach, using tighter stop-loss orders to limit potential losses. Others might employ more sophisticated trading algorithms designed to detect and react to unusual trading patterns indicative of manipulation. These adaptive strategies reflect a deeper understanding of the market's intricacies and an attempt to safeguard against the negative impacts of manipulative tactics.

The volatility introduced by manipulation also impacts long-term investment strategies. Investors who might otherwise hold Bitcoin for extended periods may be tempted to engage in short-term trading to capitalize on the frequent price swings. This shift from a buy-and-hold strategy to a more active trading approach can increase market volatility, as more participants engage in frequent buying and selling. Additionally, the high volatility can deter institutional investors who seek more stable and predictable investment environments, potentially limiting the overall growth and acceptance of Bitcoin as a mainstream asset class.

The constant threat of market manipulation necessitates a high level of vigilance among traders. They need to stay informed about market conditions, regulatory developments, and the activities of large market participants. Community-driven platforms and social media channels often serve as valuable resources for real-time information and analysis. However, the same platforms can also be sources of misinformation and market manipulation, further complicating the decision-making process.

In conclusion, the interplay between technical analysis, manipulative tactics, and trader behavior creates a complex and dynamic market environment for Bitcoin. Traders must navigate these challenges by adopting adaptive strategies, staying informed, and managing their emotional responses to market movements. Understanding the impact of manipulation on trader behavior is crucial for developing effective trading strategies and fostering a more resilient and informed trading community. As the market continues to evolve, ongoing education and awareness will be key to mitigating the adverse effects of manipulation and promoting a healthier trading ecosystem. In this subsection the following points are discussed:

Media and Information Control

Role of Media in Bitcoin Market

The role of media in the Bitcoin market is a powerful and multifaceted force that significantly influences investor behavior, market sentiment, and price volatility. As a decentralized and relatively new financial asset, Bitcoin relies heavily on information dissemination through various media channels, including traditional news outlets, online publications, social media platforms, and dedicated cryptocurrency forums. Each of these channels plays a crucial role in shaping public perception and, consequently, market dynamics.

Media coverage can create a significant impact on Bitcoin's price movements. Positive news, such as announcements of institutional investments, regulatory endorsements, or technological advancements, can drive bullish sentiment and lead to price increases. For instance, when large companies like Tesla announced Bitcoin purchases or when major financial institutions such as PayPal and Visa integrated Bitcoin into their services, the market responded with enthusiasm, leading to substantial price rallies. These announcements not only boost confidence among existing investors but also attract new participants to the market, further amplifying the upward momentum.

Conversely, negative news can trigger sharp declines in Bitcoin prices. Reports of regulatory crackdowns, security breaches, or critical statements from influential figures often lead to panic selling. For example, when China reiterated its ban on cryptocurrency transactions or when notable financial leaders like Warren Buffett and Jamie Dimon expressed skepticism about Bitcoin, the market experienced significant sell-offs. These instances highlight how quickly sentiment can shift based on media reports, underscoring the sensitivity of the Bitcoin market to external information.

Social media platforms, particularly Twitter, Reddit, and Telegram, have become vital in the rapid dissemination of information and rumors. These platforms allow for real-time discussions and the viral spread of news, which can have immediate effects on market behavior. Influential figures within the cryptocurrency community, such as Elon Musk or prominent crypto influencers, wield considerable power through their social media posts. A single tweet can lead to dramatic price movements, exemplified by Musk's tweets about Bitcoin and Dogecoin, which have repeatedly caused significant market fluctuations.

The role of media extends beyond news dissemination to include the spread of misinformation and speculative hype. In the cryptocurrency space, misinformation can have severe consequences, as traders and investors often rely on timely and accurate information to make decisions. False reports, rumors, and speculative articles can create misleading impressions about the market, leading to irrational trading behaviors. The phenomenon of "fake news" and unverified claims can exacerbate volatility and contribute to a cycle of boom and bust.

Hype-driven media coverage also plays a significant role in shaping market behavior. During bull markets, media outlets often amplify positive narratives, creating a feedback loop that fuels further buying frenzy. This can lead to inflated valuations and speculative bubbles. Conversely, during bear markets, negative media coverage can deepen pessimism and exacerbate selling pressure. This cyclical influence of media coverage contributes to the characteristic volatility of the Bitcoin market.

Moreover, media narratives can shape long-term perceptions and adoption trends. In-depth analyses, investigative reports, and educational content help demystify Bitcoin and blockchain technology for the general public. By providing a balanced view of the opportunities and risks associated with Bitcoin, media outlets can contribute to informed decision-making among investors. Educational articles and expert opinions help build a more knowledgeable investor base, which is crucial for the maturation of the market.

Regulatory news and developments are another critical aspect of media influence. Reports on regulatory changes, government policies, and legal decisions can have far-reaching implications for the Bitcoin market. For instance, the introduction of cryptocurrency regulations in major economies, such as the United States or the European Union, can create uncertainty or clarity, depending on the nature of the regulations. Media coverage of these regulatory developments helps investors understand the evolving legal landscape and adjust their strategies accordingly.

In addition to traditional and social media, dedicated cryptocurrency news platforms and forums play a vital role in the information ecosystem. Websites like CoinDesk, CoinTelegraph, and forums such as Bitcointalk provide specialized coverage of industry developments, technical analysis, and market insights. These platforms cater specifically to the cryptocurrency community, offering detailed and technical content that may not be covered by mainstream media. As a result, they serve as critical resources for traders and investors seeking in-depth information.

In conclusion, the media's role in the Bitcoin market is multifaceted, encompassing news dissemination, sentiment shaping, misinformation spread, and educational outreach. The influence of media on Bitcoin's price volatility and market dynamics underscores the importance of information in the cryptocurrency space. As the market continues to evolve, the interplay between media coverage and market behavior will remain a defining feature of Bitcoin's journey, highlighting the need for critical consumption of information and vigilant awareness of the media's power to sway market sentiment.

Misinformation and Its Effects

Misinformation in the Bitcoin market has profound effects on investor behavior, market dynamics, and the overall perception of cryptocurrencies. As a relatively new and complex financial asset, Bitcoin is particularly susceptible to the spread of false information, which can significantly influence its volatile price movements and market sentiment.

Misinformation can take various forms, including false news reports, misleading social media posts, and manipulated data. These can create confusion and uncertainty among investors, leading to irrational trading decisions. For instance, a fabricated news article claiming that a major country has banned Bitcoin can trigger a massive sell-off, causing the price to plummet. Conversely, false reports of a large corporation adopting Bitcoin as a payment method can lead to a buying frenzy, driving the price up. The rapid dissemination of such information through social media platforms amplifies its impact, as traders often react quickly to news without verifying its authenticity.

Social media plays a pivotal role in the spread of misinformation. Platforms like Twitter, Reddit, and Telegram are hotspots for cryptocurrency discussions, where news and rumors spread rapidly. Influential figures in the crypto community, often referred to as "crypto influencers," can unintentionally or deliberately spread misinformation to their large followings. A single tweet from a prominent figure can cause significant price fluctuations, as was seen with Elon Musk's tweets about Bitcoin and Dogecoin. The viral nature of social media means that misinformation can reach a vast audience quickly, exacerbating its effects on the market.

Misinformation can also arise from within the cryptocurrency community itself. Traders and investors sometimes spread false information to manipulate the market for their benefit. This practice, known as "shilling," involves promoting a particular cryptocurrency or spreading rumors to influence its price. For example, an individual might falsely claim that a specific altcoin is about to be listed on a major exchange, prompting others to buy in anticipation and driving up the price. The shiller can then sell their holdings at a profit once the price has increased, leaving other investors with losses when the truth emerges.

The impact of misinformation extends beyond short-term price movements. It can also shape long-term perceptions and beliefs about Bitcoin and the broader cryptocurrency market. Persistent misinformation can undermine confidence in Bitcoin as a reliable store of value and medium of exchange. For instance, repeated false claims about Bitcoin's environmental impact can deter environmentally conscious investors and lead to negative public perception. Similarly, misinformation about the security and legality of Bitcoin can create apprehension among potential investors, slowing down adoption and integration into mainstream financial systems.

Regulatory responses to misinformation are also significant. Governments and regulatory bodies are increasingly recognizing the need to address the spread of false information in the cryptocurrency market. Some jurisdictions have introduced measures to combat misinformation, such as requiring more transparency from cryptocurrency exchanges and implementing stricter regulations on social media platforms to monitor and control the spread of false information. However, the decentralized and global nature of the cryptocurrency market makes it challenging to enforce these measures uniformly.

Misinformation can also affect the development and implementation of regulations. Policymakers may base their decisions on inaccurate or incomplete information, leading to regulations that do not effectively address the real issues within the cryptocurrency market. For instance, overestimating the extent of illegal activities associated with Bitcoin due to misinformation can result in overly restrictive regulations that stifle innovation and legitimate use cases.

Investors can protect themselves from the effects of misinformation by adopting a critical and cautious approach to news and social media posts. Conducting thorough research, verifying information from multiple credible sources, and avoiding impulsive trading decisions based on unverified reports are essential practices. Additionally, following reputable news outlets and analysts who provide well-researched and balanced views on the cryptocurrency market can help investors make more informed decisions.

In conclusion, misinformation is a significant challenge in the Bitcoin market, influencing investor behavior, market dynamics, and regulatory responses. The rapid spread of false information through social media and other channels can lead to irrational trading decisions, volatile price movements, and long-term negative perceptions of Bitcoin. Addressing this issue requires a collective effort from regulators, the media, and the cryptocurrency community to promote transparency, accuracy, and responsible information dissemination. By being vigilant and critical consumers of information, investors can better navigate the complexities of the Bitcoin market and mitigate the impact of misinformation.

Counteracting Misinformation

Counteracting misinformation in the Bitcoin market is crucial to maintaining its integrity and ensuring that investors make well-informed decisions. The pervasive nature of misinformation can distort perceptions, drive irrational market behaviors, and lead to substantial financial losses. Thus, developing effective strategies to counteract misinformation is essential for the health and stability of the Bitcoin market.

The first step in counteracting misinformation is promoting media literacy among investors. Media literacy involves educating the public on how to critically evaluate information sources and recognize credible versus non-credible content. This education can include understanding how to identify reputable news outlets, scrutinize sensationalist headlines, and verify facts through multiple sources. By equipping investors with the skills to discern the quality of information, they can better navigate the often misleading and chaotic media landscape surrounding Bitcoin.

Reputable news organizations and cryptocurrency-focused media outlets also play a pivotal role in combating misinformation. These entities can establish and adhere to high journalistic standards, ensuring that their reporting is accurate, balanced, and thoroughly fact-checked. By providing clear, factual, and in-depth analysis, these outlets can serve as a reliable source of information, countering the false narratives often spread through less scrupulous channels. Moreover, these media organizations can debunk myths and correct false reports quickly, thereby mitigating the spread and impact of misinformation.

Social media platforms, where much of the misinformation about Bitcoin is disseminated, have a significant responsibility in this regard. Platforms like Twitter, Reddit, and Facebook can implement stricter content moderation policies and employ advanced algorithms to detect and flag false information. Collaborations with independent fact-checkers can further enhance the accuracy of information shared on these platforms. Additionally, social media companies can promote verified accounts of credible news sources and experts, ensuring that accurate information is more visible to users.

The role of blockchain technology itself in combating misinformation cannot be overstated. Blockchain's inherent properties of transparency and immutability can be leveraged to create verifiable records of transactions and statements. For instance, projects that record news articles and significant announcements on a blockchain can provide a tamper-proof archive that users can reference to verify the authenticity of information. This approach can significantly reduce the spread of altered or fabricated news.

Education and awareness campaigns are another effective strategy to counteract misinformation. Cryptocurrency exchanges, industry groups, and educational institutions can collaborate to provide comprehensive educational resources about Bitcoin and the broader cryptocurrency market. Workshops, webinars, and online courses can help demystify Bitcoin, explaining its underlying technology, market dynamics, and common misconceptions. By fostering a well-informed community, the industry can reduce the susceptibility of investors to misinformation.

Regulatory measures can also play a crucial role in addressing misinformation. Governments and regulatory bodies can introduce and enforce regulations that hold individuals and organizations accountable for spreading false information. Regulations can mandate transparency in advertising and promotions related to cryptocurrencies, ensuring that potential investors receive clear and accurate information. Furthermore, regulatory bodies can establish guidelines for media outlets and social media platforms to follow, promoting the dissemination of reliable and factual information.

Industry self-regulation and community vigilance are equally important in the fight against misinformation. Cryptocurrency communities can establish codes of conduct and best practices for information sharing. By fostering a culture of honesty and accountability, these communities can help ensure that accurate information prevails. Peer review systems, where knowledgeable community members verify and endorse credible information, can further enhance the reliability of information within these communities.

Collaborative efforts between different stakeholders—media, social platforms, regulatory bodies, and the cryptocurrency community—are essential for a comprehensive approach to counteracting misinformation. These collaborations can lead to the development of unified standards and protocols for information dissemination, creating a more transparent and trustworthy information ecosystem.

In conclusion, counteracting misinformation in the Bitcoin market requires a multifaceted approach that includes promoting media literacy, ensuring high journalistic standards, leveraging blockchain technology, conducting education and awareness campaigns, implementing regulatory measures, and fostering industry self-regulation. By adopting these strategies, the Bitcoin market can mitigate the detrimental effects of misinformation, promoting a more informed and stable trading environment. This concerted effort is essential for safeguarding the integrity of the market and supporting the continued growth and acceptance of Bitcoin as a legitimate financial asset.

Dark Pools and Off-Exchange Trading

Understanding Dark Pools

Understanding dark pools is essential to comprehending the complexities of Bitcoin trading and market dynamics. Dark pools are private financial exchanges or forums for trading securities that are not openly available to the public. These platforms allow institutional investors to trade large blocks of Bitcoin without revealing their intentions to the broader market, thus avoiding the significant price movements that such large trades might trigger on public exchanges.

Dark pools operate by providing liquidity away from the public eye. This confidentiality can be beneficial for large traders who wish to execute sizable transactions without impacting the market price. For example, if a hedge fund wants to sell a large quantity of Bitcoin, doing so on a public exchange might lead to a sharp decline in price as other traders react to the sale. By using a dark pool, the fund can sell its holdings discretely, potentially achieving a better price.

However, the opacity of dark pools raises concerns about fairness and transparency. Because these trades are not visible to the public until after they are executed, it can be difficult for other market participants to gauge the true supply and demand dynamics of Bitcoin. This lack of transparency can lead to a fragmented market, where the price on public exchanges does not accurately reflect the overall trading activity.

Dark pools contribute to the overall liquidity of the Bitcoin market, but they also present risks. The anonymity they provide can be exploited for manipulative practices. For instance, market participants might use dark pools to execute wash trades or other forms of market manipulation without detection. This can distort price signals and undermine trust in the market.

The role of dark pools in Bitcoin trading is further complicated by regulatory challenges. Traditional financial markets have established regulations to oversee dark pools and ensure they operate fairly. However, the regulatory framework for cryptocurrencies is still evolving, and oversight of dark pools in the crypto space is less stringent. This regulatory gap can create opportunities for abuse and increases the need for robust surveillance and compliance measures.

Understanding the mechanics of dark pools involves recognizing their dual nature as both a tool for achieving better trade execution and a potential avenue for manipulation. Institutional investors appreciate the ability to trade large volumes without tipping off the market, but this advantage must be balanced against the broader need for market transparency.

For individual traders and smaller investors, the existence of dark pools can seem like a double-edged sword. On one hand, they contribute to market liquidity and can help stabilize prices by absorbing large trades. On the other hand, the lack of visibility into these trades can make it harder for retail investors to make informed decisions based on the complete picture of market activity.

Efforts to mitigate the negative impacts of dark pools on market transparency include increasing regulatory oversight and developing better market surveillance tools. Regulators can enforce stricter reporting requirements for dark pool trades, ensuring that information about large transactions becomes available to the public in a timely manner. Additionally, technological advancements in market surveillance can help detect patterns indicative of manipulative behavior within dark pools.

Education and awareness are also crucial in addressing the challenges posed by dark pools. By understanding how these platforms operate and the potential risks they entail, investors can make more informed decisions. This knowledge can empower traders to recognize the signs of market manipulation and adjust their strategies accordingly.

In conclusion, dark pools play a significant role in the Bitcoin market by providing a venue for large trades to occur without causing immediate price disruptions. While they offer benefits in terms of liquidity and trade execution, their lack of transparency poses challenges for market fairness and integrity. Balancing the advantages of dark pools with the need for greater transparency and robust regulatory oversight is essential for ensuring a fair and stable Bitcoin market. As the cryptocurrency market continues to evolve, addressing the complexities of dark pools will remain a key focus for regulators, market participants, and the broader financial community.

Off-Exchange Trading Mechanisms

Off-exchange trading mechanisms play a crucial role in the cryptocurrency market, offering an alternative to traditional exchange-based trading. These mechanisms, which include over-the-counter (OTC) trading, peer-to-peer (P2P) platforms, and decentralized exchanges (DEXs), provide unique benefits and challenges for Bitcoin traders and investors.

OTC trading is a popular method for large-volume Bitcoin transactions. It involves direct trading between two parties, typically facilitated by a broker or a trading desk. This method allows traders to execute large trades without affecting the market price, as the transactions are not visible on public order books. OTC trading provides privacy and reduces the risk of slippage, making it an attractive option for institutional investors, high-net-worth individuals, and entities looking to move significant amounts of Bitcoin. However, the lack of transparency in OTC markets can lead to price discrepancies and limited price discovery, as these trades do not contribute to the public pricing mechanisms of Bitcoin.

P2P platforms offer another off-exchange trading avenue, enabling direct transactions between buyers and sellers. These platforms match users based on their trading preferences, allowing them to negotiate and settle trades without the need for intermediaries. P2P trading can provide more favorable rates, increased privacy, and access to markets in regions with limited exchange infrastructure. However, it also comes with risks such as fraud, counterparty risk, and lower liquidity compared to centralized exchanges. Effective escrow services and user rating systems are essential for mitigating these risks and ensuring secure transactions.

DEXs represent a decentralized alternative to traditional exchanges, leveraging blockchain technology to facilitate direct trading between users without intermediaries. DEXs operate through smart contracts, which automatically execute trades based on predefined conditions. This decentralized approach enhances security, reduces the risk of hacking, and aligns with the core principles of cryptocurrencies like Bitcoin. DEXs provide greater control over funds, as users retain custody of their assets throughout the trading process. However, DEXs often face challenges related to liquidity, user experience, and the complexity of smart contract interactions.

One of the significant advantages of off-exchange trading mechanisms is the ability to bypass centralized control and regulation. This can be particularly appealing in jurisdictions with restrictive regulatory environments or for individuals seeking to maintain privacy. However, this lack of regulation also introduces potential drawbacks, such as increased exposure to fraud, market manipulation, and legal uncertainties. As the cryptocurrency market matures, finding a balance between decentralization and regulatory oversight will be crucial for the sustainable growth of off-exchange trading.

The impact of off-exchange trading on market dynamics is multifaceted. On one hand, these mechanisms contribute to the overall liquidity of the Bitcoin market, facilitating large trades and enabling access to diverse trading opportunities. On the other hand, they can fragment the market, leading to price discrepancies between different trading venues. The absence of centralized price discovery in off-exchange markets can result in inefficiencies and challenges for traders trying to gauge the true market value of Bitcoin.

Regulatory perspectives on off-exchange trading vary widely across jurisdictions. Some regulators view these mechanisms with skepticism, concerned about their potential use for money laundering, tax evasion, and other illicit activities. Others recognize the innovative potential of decentralized trading and seek to create frameworks that support growth while ensuring compliance with existing financial regulations. The evolving regulatory landscape will play a significant role in shaping the future of off-exchange trading mechanisms.

In response to these challenges, industry participants are developing solutions to enhance the transparency and security of off-exchange trading. Innovations such as decentralized identity verification, reputation systems, and enhanced escrow services aim to build trust and reduce the risks associated with P2P and OTC trading. Additionally, hybrid models that combine the benefits of decentralized trading with the regulatory oversight of centralized exchanges are emerging, offering a potential middle ground.

In conclusion, off-exchange trading mechanisms are integral to the Bitcoin market, providing alternative avenues for trading and liquidity. While they offer significant advantages in terms of privacy, control, and access, they also present challenges related to transparency, security, and regulation. As the market evolves, ongoing efforts to enhance the security and efficiency of these mechanisms will be crucial for fostering a robust and inclusive trading ecosystem. Balancing the innovative potential of decentralized trading with the need for regulatory oversight will be key to ensuring the long-term stability and integrity of the Bitcoin market.

Implications for Market Integrity

The integrity of the Bitcoin market is critically impacted by the mechanisms and practices of off-exchange trading. These practices, while providing certain advantages such as liquidity and discretion, also pose significant challenges to the transparency and fairness of the market. Understanding these implications is vital for traders, investors, and regulators alike as they navigate the complexities of the cryptocurrency ecosystem.

Off-exchange trading mechanisms, including over-the-counter (OTC) transactions, peer-to-peer (P2P) platforms, and decentralized exchanges (DEXs), offer alternatives to traditional, centralized exchanges. These platforms allow large trades to be executed without the immediate price impact that would occur on a public exchange, preserving market stability for the time being. However, the opacity of these trades can lead to a lack of comprehensive market visibility, making it difficult to ascertain the true state of supply and demand at any given moment.

OTC trading desks facilitate large-volume trades directly between buyers and sellers, often through brokers. This method is favored by institutional investors and high-net-worth individuals who wish to avoid slippage—the adverse price movement that can occur when large orders are placed on public exchanges. While OTC trading contributes to market liquidity, it does so in a way that is not transparent to the broader market. This lack of visibility can lead to price discrepancies and undermine the price discovery process, as significant portions of trading activity remain hidden from the public eye.

P2P platforms, which connect buyers and sellers directly, further complicate market integrity. These platforms offer privacy and often more favorable rates, as they eliminate the need for intermediaries. However, they also pose risks such as fraud and reduced regulatory oversight. The peer-to-peer nature of these trades means that transactions are less visible and less regulated, increasing the potential for market manipulation and making it harder to enforce legal and ethical standards.

DEXs present a more technologically advanced form of off-exchange trading, using blockchain technology to facilitate direct trades between users. These exchanges enhance security and user control by removing intermediaries and using smart contracts to automate transactions. However, DEXs also face challenges related to liquidity and user experience. The decentralized nature of these exchanges can lead to fragmentation, where liquidity is spread thin across multiple platforms, reducing the overall efficiency and effectiveness of the market.

The implications of off-exchange trading for market integrity are profound. One significant concern is the potential for market manipulation. Because off-exchange trades are not immediately visible to the broader market, large players can use these platforms to execute strategies that might be considered manipulative if conducted on a public exchange. For example, they could accumulate or dispose of large positions without tipping off the market, later causing significant price movements when these actions eventually come to light.

Moreover, the lack of transparency in off-exchange trading can undermine trust in the market. Retail investors and smaller market participants, who rely on public information to make trading decisions, may find themselves at a disadvantage compared to institutional players with access to private trading avenues. This asymmetry can lead to a perception of unfairness and deter broader participation in the market.

Regulatory responses to these challenges vary. Some jurisdictions have begun to implement measures to increase the transparency and accountability of off-exchange trading. These measures include enhanced reporting requirements for OTC desks and tighter scrutiny of P2P platforms. However, the global and decentralized nature of the cryptocurrency market makes it difficult to enforce consistent regulations across all trading platforms.

In response to these challenges, the industry is exploring technological solutions to enhance transparency and market integrity. Blockchain technology itself offers potential solutions, such as using decentralized ledgers to record and verify trades in real-time, even those conducted off-exchange. Such innovations could provide a balance between the privacy and liquidity benefits of off-exchange trading and the transparency needed for a fair and efficient market.

Investor education and awareness are also crucial in mitigating the risks associated with off-exchange trading. By understanding the mechanics and risks of these trading mechanisms, investors can make more informed decisions and develop strategies to protect themselves against potential manipulation and fraud.

In conclusion, while off-exchange trading mechanisms offer valuable benefits, they also pose significant challenges to the integrity of the Bitcoin market. Ensuring that these mechanisms operate fairly and transparently is essential for the long-term health and stability of the market. As the cryptocurrency market continues to evolve, balancing the benefits of decentralized trading with the need for regulatory oversight and transparency will be critical for fostering a more inclusive and trustworthy financial ecosystem.

Chapter 5: Regulatory Perspectives and Challenges

Current Regulatory Landscape

Global Regulatory Environment

The global regulatory environment for Bitcoin and other cryptocurrencies is complex and rapidly evolving. As governments and financial authorities worldwide grapple with the challenges posed by this new form of digital asset, their approaches vary significantly, reflecting diverse economic, legal, and cultural contexts. Understanding these regulatory landscapes is crucial for investors, traders, and all stakeholders involved in the Bitcoin market.

Bitcoin's decentralized nature presents a fundamental challenge to traditional regulatory frameworks. Unlike conventional financial assets, Bitcoin operates without a central authority, making it difficult for regulators to exert control. This decentralization, while offering numerous benefits such as resistance to censorship and government intervention, also complicates efforts to implement consistent regulatory standards. Different countries have adopted varying strategies to address these challenges, ranging from outright bans to the development of comprehensive regulatory frameworks.

In the United States, the regulatory approach to Bitcoin is fragmented, involving multiple federal and state agencies. The Securities and Exchange Commission (SEC) focuses on whether cryptocurrencies qualify as securities, thus subject to its regulations. Meanwhile, the Commodity Futures Trading Commission (CFTC) classifies Bitcoin as a commodity, overseeing its trading on futures markets. The Financial Crimes Enforcement Network (FinCEN) imposes anti-money laundering (AML) and know-your-customer (KYC) requirements on cryptocurrency exchanges. State-level regulations add another layer of complexity, with some states like New York implementing stringent licensing requirements through initiatives like the BitLicense.

The European Union (EU) has been proactive in developing a cohesive regulatory framework for cryptocurrencies. The EU's Fifth Anti-Money Laundering Directive (5AMLD) extended AML and KYC obligations to cryptocurrency exchanges and wallet providers, aiming to curb illicit activities. More recently, the EU proposed the Markets in Crypto-Assets Regulation (MiCA), which seeks to create a harmonized regulatory framework across member states. MiCA aims to enhance consumer protection, ensure financial stability, and promote innovation within the crypto space by providing clear rules for issuers and service providers.

China's regulatory stance on Bitcoin has been one of strict control and periodic crackdowns. Initially embracing blockchain technology, China later imposed stringent regulations on cryptocurrency trading and mining. In 2021, the government intensified its efforts, effectively banning all domestic cryptocurrency transactions and shutting down Bitcoin mining operations. This aggressive regulatory approach aims to prevent financial risks and maintain control over the financial system, reflecting broader concerns about capital flight and financial stability.

In contrast, Japan has adopted a more progressive stance, recognizing Bitcoin as legal property and establishing a regulatory framework to oversee cryptocurrency exchanges. The Payment Services Act requires exchanges to register with the Financial Services Agency (FSA), adhere to AML and KYC regulations, and implement robust security measures to protect users' assets. Japan's regulatory environment aims to foster innovation while ensuring consumer protection and financial stability.

Singapore has emerged as a global hub for cryptocurrency innovation, thanks to its favorable regulatory environment. The Monetary Authority of Singapore (MAS) regulates cryptocurrency exchanges under the Payment Services Act, which imposes licensing requirements and AML/KYC obligations. Singapore's approach balances regulation with a supportive environment for fintech innovation, attracting numerous blockchain startups and cryptocurrency businesses.

In developing economies, the regulatory landscape is often less defined. Countries such as Nigeria and India have witnessed significant interest in Bitcoin despite ambiguous or hostile regulatory stances. In Nigeria, the Central Bank prohibited financial institutions from facilitating cryptocurrency transactions, yet peer-to-peer trading flourishes, highlighting the tension between regulatory efforts and grassroots adoption. India's regulatory environment has been marked by uncertainty, with proposed bans and regulatory frameworks creating confusion among investors and businesses.

International regulatory cooperation is increasingly recognized as crucial for addressing the challenges posed by Bitcoin and other cryptocurrencies. Organizations such as the Financial Action Task Force (FATF) have issued guidelines to enhance global AML and KYC standards for crypto assets. The FATF's "travel rule" requires exchanges to share information about the identities of participants in transactions exceeding a certain threshold, aiming to combat money laundering and terrorist financing.

As the Bitcoin market continues to grow and evolve, regulatory approaches will likely become more sophisticated and coordinated. The development of clear, consistent, and balanced regulatory frameworks is essential for fostering a secure and stable environment for Bitcoin and other cryptocurrencies. Such frameworks must address the unique characteristics of these digital assets while promoting innovation and protecting consumers.

The future of Bitcoin regulation will hinge on finding the right balance between control and innovation. Effective regulation can enhance market integrity, protect investors, and mitigate risks without stifling technological advancement. Policymakers must stay informed about technological developments and adapt their approaches to the dynamic nature of the cryptocurrency market. Engaging with industry stakeholders, fostering public-private partnerships, and encouraging international cooperation will be key to crafting regulatory frameworks that support the sustainable growth of the Bitcoin market.

Major Regulatory Bodies

The global regulatory landscape for Bitcoin is shaped by several major regulatory bodies, each playing a critical role in overseeing and shaping the rules and guidelines that govern the use and trading of cryptocurrencies. These bodies work within their respective jurisdictions and sometimes collaborate internationally to address the multifaceted challenges posed by Bitcoin and other digital assets.

In the United States, the regulatory framework for Bitcoin is primarily governed by three major bodies: the Securities and Exchange Commission (SEC), the Commodity Futures Trading Commission (CFTC), and the Financial Crimes Enforcement Network (FinCEN). The SEC's role is to oversee securities markets, and it has been crucial in determining which cryptocurrencies qualify as securities, thus falling under its regulatory purview. The CFTC, on the other hand, classifies Bitcoin as a commodity and oversees its trading in futures markets, ensuring fair and transparent trading practices. FinCEN focuses on preventing money laundering and terrorist financing, imposing AML (anti-money laundering) and KYC (know your customer) requirements on cryptocurrency exchanges and other financial institutions dealing with Bitcoin.

The European Union has taken significant steps to regulate Bitcoin through its comprehensive framework aimed at ensuring market integrity and consumer protection. The European

Securities and Markets Authority (ESMA) plays a vital role in overseeing the securities markets, including the trading of cryptocurrencies. ESMA works alongside the European Banking Authority (EBA) and the European Central Bank (ECB) to develop cohesive regulations that address the unique challenges of Bitcoin. The Markets in Crypto-Assets Regulation (MiCA) is a recent initiative by the EU that seeks to establish a harmonized regulatory environment for cryptocurrencies across member states, providing clarity and consistency for market participants.

Japan has been at the forefront of cryptocurrency regulation, with the Financial Services Agency (FSA) implementing stringent guidelines to ensure the security and stability of the market. The FSA requires cryptocurrency exchanges to register and adhere to robust AML and cybersecurity measures, making Japan one of the most regulated environments for Bitcoin trading. This proactive approach has fostered a relatively secure and transparent market, attracting numerous crypto businesses to the region.

China's approach to Bitcoin regulation has been marked by strict controls and periodic crackdowns. The People's Bank of China (PBOC) has led efforts to ban cryptocurrency trading and mining activities, citing concerns over financial stability and capital flight. Despite these restrictions, China remains a significant player in the global Bitcoin market, particularly in terms of mining activities conducted through various means to circumvent government bans.

Singapore has positioned itself as a global hub for cryptocurrency innovation, with the Monetary Authority of Singapore (MAS) providing a supportive yet regulated environment for Bitcoin businesses. The Payment Services Act governs cryptocurrency exchanges and requires them to obtain licenses, comply with AML regulations, and ensure robust consumer protection measures. This balanced approach has made Singapore an attractive destination for blockchain startups and crypto investors.

In addition to these national regulatory bodies, international organizations play a crucial role in shaping the global regulatory environment for Bitcoin. The Financial Action Task Force (FATF) is one such organization that sets international standards for AML and counter-terrorist financing (CTF) measures. The FATF has developed guidelines for the cryptocurrency sector, including the "travel rule," which requires exchanges to share customer information for transactions above a certain threshold. These guidelines aim to prevent illicit activities and ensure that cryptocurrencies are not used to facilitate crime.

Another important international entity is the International Organization of Securities Commissions (IOSCO), which provides a global forum for regulatory cooperation and sets standards for securities regulation. IOSCO's principles and guidelines help harmonize regulatory approaches across jurisdictions, fostering a more consistent and effective regulatory environment for Bitcoin and other digital assets.

The International Monetary Fund (IMF) and the World Bank also contribute to the regulatory landscape by providing policy advice and technical assistance to countries developing their cryptocurrency regulations. These organizations emphasize the importance of balancing innovation with financial stability and consumer protection, advocating for a measured approach to regulation.

The major regulatory bodies and international organizations collectively shape the evolving landscape of Bitcoin regulation. Their efforts to develop comprehensive, balanced, and effective regulatory frameworks are crucial for addressing the challenges and risks associated with Bitcoin while fostering an environment that supports innovation and growth. As the Bitcoin market continues to mature, the role of these regulatory bodies will be pivotal in ensuring that the market operates with integrity, transparency, and fairness, benefiting all participants.

Recent Regulatory Developments

Recent regulatory developments in the Bitcoin market have been driven by the rapid growth of the cryptocurrency industry and the increasing recognition of both its potential and its risks. Governments and regulatory bodies around the world have been striving to develop frameworks that balance the need for innovation with the imperative of safeguarding market integrity, investor protection, and financial stability.

In the United States, the regulatory landscape has seen significant evolution. The Securities and Exchange Commission (SEC) has intensified its scrutiny of cryptocurrency markets, focusing on initial coin offerings (ICOs) and other digital asset transactions that may qualify as securities. The SEC's enforcement actions have included high-profile cases against companies and individuals for fraudulent and unregistered ICOs, signaling a stringent stance on compliance with securities laws. The Commodity Futures Trading Commission (CFTC) has also been active, overseeing Bitcoin futures markets and addressing cases of market manipulation. Additionally, the Financial Crimes Enforcement Network (FinCEN) has updated its guidance to emphasize that AML and KYC regulations apply to cryptocurrency exchanges and wallet providers, reinforcing the need for robust compliance measures.

The European Union has been proactive in its regulatory approach, aiming to create a harmonized framework for cryptocurrencies across member states. The proposed Markets in Crypto-Assets Regulation (MiCA) is a landmark development, designed to provide legal clarity and consumer protection while fostering innovation. MiCA covers a wide range of digital assets, setting out requirements for issuers and service providers, including those involved in stablecoins and other significant digital tokens. This regulation aims to prevent market abuse, ensure financial stability, and enhance the overall security of the crypto ecosystem within the EU.

China's regulatory developments have been characterized by a stringent and often restrictive approach. In recent years, the Chinese government has imposed comprehensive bans on cryptocurrency trading and mining activities. These actions reflect concerns over financial stability, capital outflows, and environmental impacts associated with Bitcoin mining. Despite these measures, China remains a key player in the global Bitcoin market, with many activities moving offshore or operating through decentralized platforms that are harder to regulate.

Japan has continued to refine its regulatory framework to maintain its position as a leading hub for cryptocurrency innovation. The Financial Services Agency (FSA) has implemented rigorous standards for cryptocurrency exchanges, including stringent AML and KYC requirements, cybersecurity measures, and regular audits. These regulations are designed to protect consumers and ensure the integrity of the financial system, while also promoting the growth of the crypto industry. Recent amendments to the Payment Services Act have further clarified the legal status of cryptocurrencies and introduced additional safeguards for investors.

Singapore has solidified its reputation as a crypto-friendly jurisdiction with the implementation of the Payment Services Act. The Monetary Authority of Singapore (MAS) oversees the licensing and regulation of cryptocurrency exchanges, ensuring compliance with AML and CTF (counter-terrorist financing) requirements. MAS has also been actively engaging with industry stakeholders to develop balanced regulations that support innovation while addressing potential risks. Singapore's approach has attracted numerous blockchain startups and established a vibrant ecosystem for digital assets.

In developing economies, regulatory responses to Bitcoin have been mixed. Countries like Nigeria and India have experienced significant public interest in cryptocurrencies, despite regulatory uncertainties. Nigeria's central bank initially banned financial institutions from facilitating cryptocurrency transactions, but the country has seen robust peer-to-peer trading activity. In India, the regulatory environment has been marked by ambiguity, with the government considering various approaches, including potential bans and regulatory frameworks to harness the benefits of blockchain technology while mitigating associated risks.

International organizations have also played a pivotal role in shaping the regulatory environment for Bitcoin. The Financial Action Task Force (FATF) has updated its guidelines to include cryptocurrencies, emphasizing the need for member countries to implement AML and CTF measures. The FATF's "travel rule" requires cryptocurrency exchanges to share customer information for transactions above a certain threshold, aiming to prevent money laundering and terrorist financing. The International Monetary Fund (IMF) and the World Bank have provided policy advice and technical assistance to countries developing their cryptocurrency regulations, advocating for a balanced approach that supports innovation while ensuring financial stability.

Technological advancements and industry best practices are emerging as crucial elements in the regulatory landscape. Blockchain analytics firms are developing tools to enhance transparency and traceability of transactions, aiding regulators and compliance teams in detecting and preventing illicit activities. Decentralized finance (DeFi) platforms and decentralized exchanges (DEXs) present new regulatory challenges and opportunities, prompting ongoing discussions about how to effectively integrate these innovations into existing regulatory frameworks.

In conclusion, recent regulatory developments in the Bitcoin market reflect a global effort to balance the benefits of innovation with the need for market integrity, consumer protection, and financial stability. As the cryptocurrency industry continues to evolve, regulatory approaches will need to adapt to address emerging risks and opportunities. Collaboration among national regulators, international organizations, and industry stakeholders will be essential to creating a cohesive and effective regulatory environment that supports the sustainable growth of the Bitcoin market and the broader digital asset ecosystem.

Challenges in Regulating Bitcoin

Decentralization vs. Regulation

The interplay between decentralization and regulation in the context of Bitcoin represents one of the most intriguing and complex aspects of the cryptocurrency's existence. Bitcoin, by design, is a decentralized digital currency, free from the control of any central authority. This decentralization is both its greatest strength and a source of significant challenges, particularly when it comes to regulation.

Decentralization is central to Bitcoin's identity. Satoshi Nakamoto's vision for Bitcoin was to create a peer-to-peer electronic cash system that operates without the need for intermediaries such as banks or governments. Transactions are verified by network nodes through cryptography and recorded in a public distributed ledger called a blockchain. This system is designed to be secure, transparent, and resistant to censorship. The fixed supply of 21 million bitcoins further underscores its decentralized ethos, providing a safeguard against inflationary practices often seen with fiat currencies.

However, the very features that make Bitcoin attractive also complicate efforts to regulate it. Traditional financial systems are built around centralized control, where regulatory bodies can enforce laws, impose sanctions, and ensure compliance with financial regulations. Bitcoin's decentralized nature makes it difficult for any single entity to exert such control. This lack of central authority raises significant questions about how to effectively regulate Bitcoin to prevent misuse while preserving its foundational principles.

Regulatory bodies around the world have taken varying approaches to address this challenge. Some countries have embraced Bitcoin, recognizing its potential for innovation and economic growth. For instance, in the United States, regulatory agencies like the SEC and CFTC have been working to create a framework that allows for the growth of cryptocurrency markets while protecting investors. These agencies have focused on issues such as securities fraud, market manipulation, and the application of AML and KYC laws to cryptocurrency exchanges.

In contrast, other countries have taken a more restrictive approach. China, for example, has imposed stringent regulations, including banning cryptocurrency trading and mining activities. The Chinese government's stance reflects concerns over financial stability and the potential for capital flight. Despite these restrictions, the decentralized nature of Bitcoin means that enforcement can be challenging, and activities often continue through decentralized exchanges or offshore entities.

The tension between decentralization and regulation is further highlighted by the rise of decentralized finance (DeFi). DeFi platforms aim to replicate traditional financial services such as lending, borrowing, and trading on blockchain networks without intermediaries. While DeFi presents opportunities for financial inclusion and innovation, it also poses significant regulatory challenges. The anonymity and lack of oversight in DeFi can facilitate illicit activities such as money laundering and fraud. Regulators are thus faced with the dilemma of how to enforce compliance in a system designed to operate without centralized control.

Privacy is another critical issue at the intersection of decentralization and regulation. Bitcoin transactions, while pseudonymous, can be traced on the blockchain, allowing for some degree of transparency. However, privacy-focused cryptocurrencies like Monero and Zcash offer enhanced anonymity features that complicate regulatory efforts. These privacy coins are designed to obscure transaction details, making it difficult for regulators to track illicit activities. The use of such technologies underscores the need for a balanced approach that respects individual privacy while ensuring regulatory oversight.

Jurisdictional conflicts add another layer of complexity. Bitcoin operates on a global scale, transcending national borders. This global reach means that regulatory actions in one country can have ripple effects worldwide. For instance, when China announced its crackdown on cryptocurrency mining, it had a significant impact on the global hash rate and Bitcoin's price. Coordinating regulatory efforts across jurisdictions is therefore essential but challenging. International organizations like the Financial Action Task Force (FATF) play a crucial role in developing global standards for cryptocurrency regulation, but implementing these standards consistently across different legal and regulatory environments remains a formidable task.

Despite these challenges, there are potential pathways for reconciling decentralization with effective regulation. One approach is the development of technology-driven regulatory solutions. Blockchain analytics tools, for example, can enhance transparency and help regulators monitor transactions without compromising the decentralized nature of cryptocurrencies. These tools can identify patterns of suspicious activity and trace the flow of funds, providing valuable insights for regulatory enforcement.

Another approach is fostering greater industry collaboration. Engaging with stakeholders from the cryptocurrency industry, including developers, exchanges, and advocacy groups, can help regulators understand the nuances of the technology and develop more informed policies. Public-private partnerships can also play a key role in addressing regulatory challenges and promoting innovation.

In conclusion, the tension between decentralization and regulation in the Bitcoin ecosystem is a defining feature of its evolution. Balancing the need for regulatory oversight with the principles of decentralization is essential for ensuring the long-term viability and integrity of the cryptocurrency market. As the landscape continues to evolve, a nuanced and adaptive approach will be necessary to navigate the complexities and realize the full potential of Bitcoin and other decentralized technologies.

Anonymity and Privacy Issues

The dichotomy of Bitcoin's inherent promise of anonymity and privacy against the regulatory imperatives of transparency and accountability forms a complex and contentious issue. Bitcoin was originally designed to offer a degree of pseudonymity, allowing users to transact without revealing their identities directly. Transactions are recorded on a public ledger, the blockchain, which does not inherently contain personal information. Instead, it links transactions to cryptographic addresses, providing a layer of privacy while maintaining transparency of the transaction history.

However, the pseudonymous nature of Bitcoin is not absolute. While addresses are not directly linked to personal identities, they can be traced and analyzed through various means. Sophisticated blockchain analysis tools have been developed to track and deanonymize transactions, linking them to real-world identities. This capability has significant implications for privacy and regulatory compliance, raising critical questions about the balance between individual privacy rights and the need for regulatory oversight to prevent illicit activities.

The privacy afforded by Bitcoin has attracted a diverse group of users, including those seeking to protect their financial privacy from overreaching government surveillance, and those engaging in illegal activities such as money laundering, tax evasion, and the financing of terrorism. This duality has prompted a regulatory backlash, as governments and financial regulators seek to impose measures that ensure Bitcoin transactions do not facilitate criminal activities. The challenge lies in implementing regulations that deter illegal use without undermining the legitimate privacy interests of law-abiding users.

Regulatory bodies worldwide have been grappling with how to address the anonymity provided by Bitcoin. The Financial Action Task Force (FATF) has been at the forefront, recommending that countries implement regulations that require cryptocurrency exchanges to follow Anti-Money Laundering (AML) and Know

Your Customer (KYC) protocols. These regulations necessitate that exchanges collect and verify the identities of their users, thereby reducing the anonymity of Bitcoin transactions. The FATF's "travel rule" further requires that financial institutions share customer information when transferring digital assets, ensuring traceability across platforms.

The European Union has also taken significant steps in this direction with the Fifth Anti-Money Laundering Directive (5AMLD), which extends AML and KYC requirements to cryptocurrency exchanges and wallet providers. This directive mandates that these entities verify the identities of their customers and report suspicious activities, thereby increasing transparency and reducing the potential for anonymous misuse. However, these measures have been met with resistance from privacy advocates who argue that they erode the foundational privacy aspects of Bitcoin and other cryptocurrencies.

In the United States, regulatory bodies such as the Financial Crimes Enforcement Network (FinCEN) have implemented similar requirements, compelling cryptocurrency exchanges to comply with AML and KYC regulations. These measures are designed to prevent illicit use of cryptocurrencies while maintaining the integrity of the financial system. Nonetheless, the tension between privacy and regulation remains palpable, with ongoing debates about the appropriate level of oversight.

Amid these regulatory developments, privacy-focused cryptocurrencies like Monero, Zcash, and Dash have gained popularity. These cryptocurrencies offer enhanced privacy features, such as stealth addresses, ring signatures, and zero-knowledge proofs, which obscure transaction details and make it difficult to trace the flow of funds. While these technologies provide robust privacy protections for users, they also pose significant challenges for regulators. The use of such privacy coins complicates efforts to track and prevent illegal activities, prompting some jurisdictions to consider outright bans or restrictions on their use.

The rise of decentralized finance (DeFi) further complicates the landscape. DeFi platforms operate without intermediaries, providing financial services such as lending, borrowing, and trading on decentralized networks. These platforms often lack the centralized entities that regulators can target for compliance, making it challenging to enforce AML and KYC regulations. As DeFi continues to grow, finding a balance between fostering innovation and ensuring regulatory compliance will be crucial.

Privacy-enhancing technologies and regulations are not inherently incompatible. Innovative solutions such as zero-knowledge proofs and privacy-preserving cryptographic techniques offer the potential to enhance privacy while enabling compliance with regulatory requirements. For example, zero-knowledge proofs can allow users to prove the legitimacy of transactions without revealing underlying details, providing a way to satisfy regulatory demands for transparency without compromising user privacy.

Ultimately, the balance between decentralization and regulation, anonymity and transparency, remains a dynamic and evolving issue. As Bitcoin and other cryptocurrencies continue to mature, the interplay between technological advancements and regulatory frameworks will shape the future of financial privacy. It is imperative to find a middle ground that respects individual privacy rights while preventing the misuse of cryptocurrencies for illegal activities. This balance will ensure the sustainable growth of the cryptocurrency ecosystem, maintaining its integrity and trustworthiness in the eyes of users and regulators alike.

Jurisdictional Conflicts

The clash between decentralized cryptocurrencies and the regulatory frameworks imposed by various jurisdictions has become one of the most contentious issues in the digital financial ecosystem. Bitcoin, as the pioneering cryptocurrency, has especially highlighted the challenges of operating a global financial asset that inherently resists centralized control. Jurisdictional conflicts arise when different countries adopt divergent regulatory stances, each reflecting their unique financial policies, economic goals, and security concerns.

One of the primary sources of conflict is the varying definitions and legal classifications of Bitcoin. Some countries, like Japan, have embraced Bitcoin as a legitimate form of payment, integrating it into their financial systems with clear regulatory guidelines. In contrast, nations like China have imposed stringent restrictions, banning cryptocurrency exchanges and mining operations outright. These conflicting approaches create a fragmented regulatory environment, complicating compliance for global businesses and individuals operating in multiple jurisdictions.

The United States presents a microcosm of these jurisdictional conflicts. Different federal and state agencies offer varied perspectives on Bitcoin. The Securities and Exchange Commission (SEC) classifies certain cryptocurrency offerings as securities, subjecting them to specific regulatory requirements. The Commodity Futures Trading Commission (CFTC), however, views Bitcoin as a commodity, regulating its trading under a different set of rules. This lack of a unified regulatory approach can lead to confusion and increased compliance costs for market participants.

The European Union has attempted to harmonize its approach through regulations like the Markets in Crypto-Assets (MiCA) proposal, aiming to create a cohesive framework across member states. However, individual countries within the EU still maintain some autonomy, leading to potential discrepancies in implementation and enforcement. This dual-layered regulatory environment illustrates the complexity of achieving uniform oversight in a region with diverse economic priorities and regulatory philosophies.

The issue of cross-border transactions further exacerbates jurisdictional conflicts. Bitcoin's decentralized nature allows for seamless, borderless transactions, which can bypass traditional financial systems. This characteristic, while advantageous for efficiency and inclusivity, poses significant challenges for regulators aiming to enforce anti-money laundering (AML) and counter-terrorist financing (CTF) measures. For instance, a transaction originating in a jurisdiction with strict regulatory oversight might end up in a country with lax or nonexistent cryptocurrency regulations, complicating enforcement efforts.

To address these challenges, international cooperation and standardized regulatory frameworks are essential. The Financial Action Task Force (FATF) has been instrumental in this regard, issuing guidelines that encourage countries to adopt consistent AML and CTF measures for cryptocurrencies. The FATF's travel rule, which mandates the sharing of customer information between financial institutions during transactions, seeks to enhance transparency and traceability. However, implementing such standards uniformly across diverse legal and regulatory landscapes remains a formidable task.

The rise of decentralized finance (DeFi) platforms and decentralized autonomous organizations (DAOs) introduces additional layers of complexity. These entities operate without centralized control, further challenging traditional regulatory models. For instance, a DeFi platform could facilitate financial services globally without adhering to any single country's regulatory requirements. This decentralized operation raises significant questions about accountability, compliance, and enforcement.

Privacy concerns also play a pivotal role in jurisdictional conflicts. Regulations that mandate the collection and sharing of user data, like the General Data Protection Regulation (GDPR) in the EU, may conflict with the pseudonymous nature of Bitcoin transactions. Balancing the need for privacy with the requirements for regulatory compliance presents an ongoing challenge. Privacy-enhancing technologies, such as zero-knowledge proofs, offer potential solutions by allowing the verification of transaction legitimacy without revealing underlying data, but their adoption and integration into regulatory frameworks are still in nascent stages.

Jurisdictional conflicts are not solely limited to regulatory measures but also extend to taxation policies. Different countries have adopted varying tax treatments for Bitcoin transactions, ranging from capital gains taxes to transaction-specific levies. This diversity creates a complex tax compliance environment for individuals and businesses engaged in cross-border activities. Harmonizing tax policies related to cryptocurrencies remains a critical issue that requires international collaboration and negotiation.

The evolving geopolitical landscape adds another dimension to jurisdictional conflicts. Countries may leverage their regulatory stances on Bitcoin as part of broader economic or strategic goals. For instance, nations aiming to undermine the dominance of the U.S. dollar in international trade may adopt more favorable regulations for Bitcoin and other cryptocurrencies, positioning themselves as attractive hubs for digital finance. Conversely, countries seeking to protect their fiat currencies and traditional financial institutions may impose restrictive measures to curb the adoption of Bitcoin.

In conclusion, the jurisdictional conflicts surrounding Bitcoin highlight the inherent tensions between a decentralized financial asset and the traditional, geographically-bound regulatory frameworks. Addressing these conflicts requires a nuanced and collaborative approach, balancing the benefits of innovation and financial inclusion with the imperatives of security, transparency, and compliance. As the cryptocurrency landscape continues to evolve, fostering international cooperation and developing adaptive regulatory models will be crucial for navigating the complexities of this global financial revolution.

Future of Bitcoin Regulation

Potential Regulatory Models

The ongoing regulatory discourse surrounding Bitcoin and other cryptocurrencies often finds itself at the crossroads of decentralization and the quest for a coherent regulatory framework. As governments and financial institutions grapple with the unprecedented nature of decentralized digital currencies, potential regulatory models emerge, each aiming to balance innovation with the need for oversight and protection.

One potential regulatory model is the adoption of comprehensive frameworks similar to those used for traditional financial markets. This approach would involve classifying Bitcoin and other cryptocurrencies under existing securities or commodities laws, thus subjecting them to the same stringent requirements as traditional financial instruments. This model seeks to provide clarity and stability by ensuring that cryptocurrency exchanges and related entities adhere to established regulatory standards, such as Anti-Money Laundering (AML) and Know Your Customer (KYC) protocols. The goal is to prevent illicit activities and protect investors while maintaining market integrity.

Another model focuses on the creation of new, cryptocurrency-specific regulatory frameworks. This approach acknowledges the unique characteristics of digital currencies and aims to develop tailored regulations that address their distinct challenges and opportunities. For instance, regulators could establish dedicated agencies or divisions within existing financial oversight bodies to oversee cryptocurrency activities. These specialized entities would possess the expertise to effectively monitor and regulate the rapidly evolving crypto market, ensuring that regulations keep pace with technological advancements.

A hybrid regulatory model combines elements of both traditional and cryptocurrency-specific frameworks. This approach leverages existing regulatory infrastructure while incorporating new rules designed to address the nuances of digital currencies. Hybrid models often involve a phased implementation strategy, gradually introducing regulations to allow the market to adapt and stakeholders to provide feedback. This incremental approach helps to mitigate potential disruptions and ensures that regulations are both effective and practical.

Self-regulation represents another intriguing model, wherein the cryptocurrency industry itself takes on the responsibility of developing and enforcing standards. Industry-led initiatives, such as the establishment of self-regulatory organizations (SROs), can create a framework for best practices, ethical conduct, and compliance. SROs would work in collaboration with government regulators, providing a bridge between the industry and regulatory authorities. This model promotes industry accountability and leverages the expertise of market participants to create effective oversight mechanisms.

Decentralized governance is an innovative model that aligns closely with the ethos of cryptocurrencies. In this model, regulatory functions are distributed across the network of cryptocurrency users and stakeholders, using blockchain technology to enforce rules and ensure compliance. Decentralized autonomous organizations (DAOs) could play a pivotal role in this model, governing the ecosystem through consensus mechanisms and smart contracts. While decentralized governance presents a radically different approach to regulation, it also poses significant challenges in terms of enforcement and coordination with traditional regulatory bodies.

A risk-based regulatory approach focuses on identifying and mitigating specific risks associated with cryptocurrency activities. This model involves conducting comprehensive risk assessments to determine the areas that require regulatory intervention, such as fraud, market manipulation, and cybersecurity threats. Regulators would then develop targeted measures to address these risks without imposing unnecessary burdens on the broader market. This approach aims to balance innovation and protection, ensuring that regulations are proportionate to the risks involved.

International cooperation and harmonization are crucial components of effective cryptocurrency regulation. Given the global nature of digital currencies, unilateral regulatory actions by individual countries may prove insufficient. International regulatory bodies, such as the Financial Action Task Force

(FATF) and the International Organization of Securities Commissions (IOSCO), can play a pivotal role in fostering cooperation and developing harmonized standards. By aligning regulations across jurisdictions, regulators can enhance cross-border collaboration, reduce regulatory arbitrage, and create a more cohesive regulatory environment.

Finally, regulatory sandboxes offer a dynamic and flexible model for cryptocurrency regulation. Sandboxes provide a controlled environment where cryptocurrency projects can operate under relaxed regulatory conditions, allowing regulators to observe and understand their activities without stifling innovation. This model encourages experimentation and collaboration between regulators and industry participants, facilitating the development of effective regulatory frameworks based on real-world insights.

As the cryptocurrency landscape continues to evolve, finding the right regulatory model is essential for fostering a secure and transparent market. Each model presents unique advantages and challenges, and a one-size-fits-all approach is unlikely to be effective. A nuanced and adaptive regulatory strategy, incorporating elements from multiple models, may offer the best path forward. By balancing innovation with protection, regulators can support the growth of the cryptocurrency market while safeguarding the interests of investors and the broader financial system.

Impact of Regulation on Market

The intersection of Bitcoin and regulation brings into focus a dynamic landscape, where the impact of regulatory measures significantly shapes the market's evolution. Understanding this impact involves examining how regulatory interventions influence various facets of the Bitcoin ecosystem, from market behavior to investor sentiment and overall market stability.

Regulation plays a crucial role in shaping market dynamics by introducing rules and guidelines aimed at fostering transparency, protecting investors, and maintaining market integrity. When governments and regulatory bodies implement comprehensive regulatory frameworks, they aim to mitigate risks associated with Bitcoin trading, such as fraud, market manipulation, and financial crimes. These regulations often include requirements for Anti-Money Laundering (AML) and Know Your Customer (KYC) procedures, which mandate that exchanges and trading platforms verify the identities of their users. By enforcing these measures, regulators seek to prevent illicit activities and ensure that the market operates within the bounds of the law.

The introduction of clear regulatory guidelines can have a stabilizing effect on the Bitcoin market. Investors and traders are more likely to participate in a market where there are well-defined rules, as this reduces uncertainty and enhances trust. Regulatory clarity helps legitimize Bitcoin as an asset class, attracting institutional investors who might otherwise be wary of participating in an unregulated environment. As more institutional players enter the market, the influx of capital can contribute to reduced volatility and increased liquidity, fostering a more stable trading environment.

However, the impact of regulation is not universally positive. Overly stringent or poorly designed regulations can stifle innovation and limit the growth of the cryptocurrency market. For example, excessive regulatory burdens on exchanges and startups can increase compliance costs, driving some businesses to operate in more lenient jurisdictions or even pushing them into the unregulated, opaque corners of the market. This regulatory arbitrage can lead to fragmented markets and undermine the effectiveness of global regulatory efforts.

One of the critical challenges regulators face is striking a balance between fostering innovation and ensuring market stability. Bitcoin and other cryptocurrencies represent a technological frontier with significant potential for financial innovation. Regulations that are too restrictive can hinder the development of new financial products and services, ultimately stifling innovation. On the other hand, a lack of regulation can create an environment ripe for fraud, manipulation, and other malpractices, undermining investor confidence and market integrity.

The geographical diversity of regulatory approaches further complicates the landscape. Different countries have adopted varying stances on Bitcoin regulation, reflecting their unique economic, political, and cultural contexts. For instance, Japan has embraced Bitcoin by recognizing it as a legal payment method, while China has imposed stringent restrictions on cryptocurrency trading and mining activities. The European Union has pursued a more balanced approach, seeking to harmonize regulations across member states through initiatives like the Markets in Crypto-Assets (MiCA) regulation. These divergent approaches create a patchwork of regulatory environments, posing challenges for businesses operating internationally and complicating cross-border regulatory enforcement.

In the United States, regulatory bodies such as the Securities and Exchange Commission (SEC) and the Commodity Futures Trading Commission (CFTC) have taken active roles in overseeing Bitcoin-related activities. The SEC has focused on regulating Initial Coin Offerings (ICOs) and classifying certain cryptocurrencies as securities, subject to federal securities laws. The CFTC, on the other hand, has jurisdiction over Bitcoin futures and derivatives markets, treating Bitcoin as a commodity. This multi-agency oversight reflects the complexity of regulating a multifaceted asset like Bitcoin, where different aspects fall under the purview of various regulatory bodies.

The regulatory environment also influences market sentiment and investor behavior. Announcements of new regulations or enforcement actions can trigger significant market reactions, as investors reassess the risks and opportunities associated with Bitcoin. Positive regulatory developments, such as the approval of Bitcoin exchange-traded funds (ETFs) or the adoption of clear legal frameworks, can boost investor confidence and drive market growth. Conversely, regulatory crackdowns or negative regulatory news can lead to sharp price declines as investors flee perceived risks.

Regulatory developments can also impact the infrastructure of the Bitcoin market. Exchanges, custodians, and other service providers must adapt to comply with evolving regulations, which can lead to increased operational costs and changes in business models. For instance, exchanges may need to implement robust AML and KYC procedures, enhance cybersecurity measures, and ensure compliance with tax reporting requirements. These adjustments, while necessary for regulatory compliance, can strain resources and impact profitability.

Despite the challenges, effective regulation has the potential to enhance the long-term stability and credibility of the Bitcoin market. By addressing issues such as market manipulation, fraud, and systemic risks, regulators can create a more transparent and trustworthy environment for investors. Moreover, regulatory frameworks that encourage responsible innovation can support the growth of new financial products and services, contributing to the broader adoption of Bitcoin and other cryptocurrencies.

In conclusion, the impact of regulation on the Bitcoin market is multifaceted, encompassing both positive and negative effects. While regulation can provide stability, enhance investor protection, and legitimize the market, it can also pose challenges in terms of compliance costs, innovation constraints, and regulatory fragmentation. Striking the right balance is crucial for fostering a healthy and sustainable Bitcoin market, where the benefits of innovation can be realized without compromising market integrity and investor trust. As the regulatory landscape continues to evolve, ongoing dialogue and collaboration between regulators, industry participants, and stakeholders will be essential for navigating the complexities of this rapidly changing market.

Roadmap for Effective Regulation

In the realm of Bitcoin, where the promise of decentralization meets the reality of market manipulation, the establishment of effective regulation emerges as a critical pathway to ensuring stability and fairness. This roadmap for effective regulation of Bitcoin and other cryptocurrencies must navigate the delicate balance between fostering innovation and protecting market integrity. To achieve this, a multi-faceted approach is essential, incorporating comprehensive frameworks, international cooperation, and adaptive strategies that evolve with the market.

One of the fundamental pillars of effective regulation is the creation of clear and comprehensive regulatory frameworks. These frameworks should define the legal status of cryptocurrencies, establish guidelines for their use, and outline the responsibilities of market participants. By providing clarity, these regulations can reduce uncertainty, enhance investor confidence, and encourage the participation of institutional investors. Such frameworks should encompass Anti-Money Laundering (AML) and Know Your Customer (KYC) requirements, ensuring that exchanges and trading platforms verify user identities and monitor transactions for suspicious activities. These measures are crucial in preventing financial crimes and maintaining the integrity of the market.

International cooperation and harmonization of regulations are equally vital. Given the global nature of cryptocurrencies, inconsistent regulatory approaches across different jurisdictions can lead to regulatory arbitrage, where market participants exploit lenient regulations in certain regions. To address this, international regulatory bodies like the Financial Action Task Force (FATF) and the International Organization of Securities Commissions (IOSCO) should work towards developing standardized regulatory guidelines. These global standards can help create a cohesive regulatory environment, facilitating cross-border collaboration and enforcement.

An adaptive regulatory approach is necessary to keep pace with the rapidly evolving cryptocurrency market. Regulators must be prepared to continuously assess and update regulations in response to new developments and emerging risks. This adaptive strategy involves engaging with industry stakeholders, monitoring market trends, and conducting regular risk assessments. By maintaining an ongoing dialogue with market participants, regulators can gain valuable insights and ensure that regulations remain relevant and effective.

Self-regulation within the cryptocurrency industry can complement government regulations. Industry-led initiatives, such as the formation of self-regulatory organizations (SROs), can establish best practices, ethical standards, and compliance guidelines. These SROs can work in collaboration with government regulators, providing a bridge between the industry and regulatory authorities. Self-regulation fosters accountability and leverages the expertise of market participants to create effective oversight mechanisms.

Decentralized governance models present an innovative approach to regulation, aligning with the core principles of cryptocurrencies. In this model, regulatory functions are distributed across the network of users and stakeholders, utilizing blockchain technology to enforce rules and ensure compliance. Decentralized autonomous organizations (DAOs) could play a pivotal role in this governance structure, operating through consensus mechanisms and smart contracts. While this model poses challenges in terms of enforcement and coordination, it offers a decentralized and transparent alternative to traditional regulatory frameworks.

The use of regulatory sandboxes provides a flexible environment for innovation while ensuring regulatory oversight. These sandboxes allow cryptocurrency projects to operate under relaxed regulatory conditions, enabling regulators to observe and understand their activities without stifling innovation. By fostering experimentation and collaboration, regulatory sandboxes can help develop effective regulations based on real-world insights, balancing the need for oversight with the promotion of technological advancements.

A risk-based regulatory approach focuses on identifying and mitigating specific risks associated with cryptocurrency activities. This approach involves conducting comprehensive risk assessments to pinpoint areas requiring regulatory intervention, such as fraud, market manipulation, and cybersecurity threats. Targeted measures can then be developed to address these risks without imposing unnecessary burdens on the broader market. By tailoring regulations to the level of risk, this approach ensures proportionality and effectiveness.

Education and awareness campaigns are crucial components of a comprehensive regulatory strategy. By educating investors, traders, and the general public about the risks and benefits of cryptocurrencies, regulators can promote informed decision-making and enhance market integrity. Public awareness initiatives should cover topics such as identifying signs of market manipulation, understanding regulatory requirements, and adopting best practices for trading and investing.

Lastly, robust enforcement mechanisms are essential for ensuring compliance with regulatory frameworks. Regulators must have the authority and resources to conduct investigations, enforce regulations, and penalize non-compliance. Effective enforcement deters illicit activities and reinforces the credibility of the regulatory framework. Coordination between different regulatory bodies, both domestic and international, is necessary to address cross-border challenges and ensure comprehensive oversight.

In conclusion, the roadmap for effective regulation of Bitcoin and other cryptocurrencies requires a holistic and adaptive approach. By establishing clear regulatory frameworks, fostering international cooperation, embracing self-regulation and decentralized governance, utilizing regulatory sandboxes, adopting a risk-based approach, promoting education and awareness, and ensuring robust enforcement, regulators can create a balanced environment that nurtures innovation while safeguarding market integrity. This multifaceted strategy is essential for realizing the full potential of cryptocurrencies while addressing the challenges posed by their unique characteristics and dynamic nature.

Chapter 6: The Future of Bitcoin

Scenarios for Bitcoin's Future

Bullish Scenarios

In the constantly evolving landscape of Bitcoin, the complex interplay of market dynamics is shaped by numerous factors, with regulatory developments playing a critical role. As cryptocurrencies continue to mature, understanding the impact of recent regulatory changes is essential for investors, traders, and policymakers alike.

Regulatory bodies worldwide have been actively monitoring the growth of Bitcoin and other cryptocurrencies, recognizing both their potential and the challenges they pose. Recent years have seen a surge in regulatory initiatives aimed at bringing clarity and stability to the market. These efforts are crucial in mitigating risks such as fraud, money laundering, and market manipulation, while fostering innovation and protecting investors.

One of the significant regulatory developments is the increasing adoption of Anti-Money Laundering (AML) and Know Your Customer (KYC) regulations. Governments and regulatory bodies are implementing stringent measures to ensure that cryptocurrency exchanges and trading platforms verify the identities of their users and monitor transactions for suspicious activities. These regulations aim to curb illicit activities and enhance the overall security of the cryptocurrency ecosystem.

Additionally, the introduction of regulatory frameworks specific to cryptocurrencies has been a pivotal step. For instance, the European Union's Markets in Crypto-Assets (MiCA) regulation is designed to create a comprehensive regulatory framework for cryptocurrencies and related services within the EU. MiCA aims to provide legal certainty, protect consumers, and support the integrity of the cryptocurrency market. By establishing clear guidelines, MiCA seeks to balance innovation with investor protection.

In the United States, the Securities and Exchange Commission (SEC) and the Commodity Futures Trading Commission (CFTC) have been actively involved in regulating cryptocurrencies. The SEC's focus on determining whether certain cryptocurrencies qualify as securities has significant implications for the market. By classifying some digital assets as securities, the SEC enforces stricter disclosure and compliance requirements, which can impact the way these assets are issued and traded.

Moreover, the recent emphasis on stablecoins has highlighted the need for regulatory oversight. Stablecoins, designed to maintain a stable value by being pegged to fiat currencies or other assets, have gained popularity due to their potential to facilitate smoother transactions and reduce volatility. However, their growing use has raised concerns about their potential impact on financial stability. Regulators are exploring ways to ensure that stablecoins are adequately backed and transparent, addressing risks related to liquidity and consumer protection.

The evolving regulatory landscape also includes initiatives to address environmental concerns associated with cryptocurrency mining. Bitcoin mining, in particular, has faced criticism for its high energy consumption and environmental impact. Some jurisdictions are considering regulations to encourage the use of renewable energy sources for mining operations, while others are exploring carbon taxes and other measures to mitigate the environmental footprint of cryptocurrency mining.

International cooperation is another critical aspect of recent regulatory developments. Given the global nature of cryptocurrencies, collaboration among regulatory bodies is essential to create a harmonized regulatory environment. Organizations such as the Financial Action Task Force (FATF) are working to develop global standards for cryptocurrency regulation, promoting consistency and cooperation across borders.

While these regulatory developments aim to enhance the safety and stability of the cryptocurrency market, they also present challenges. The fast-paced nature of technological innovation in the cryptocurrency space often outstrips the ability of regulators to keep up. Striking a balance between fostering innovation and ensuring robust oversight requires continuous dialogue between regulators and industry stakeholders.

In conclusion, recent regulatory developments have significantly shaped the Bitcoin market and the broader cryptocurrency landscape. By implementing measures to enhance security, protect investors, and address environmental concerns, regulators are laying the groundwork for a more stable and transparent market. However, the dynamic nature of the cryptocurrency market necessitates ongoing adaptation and cooperation to ensure that regulations remain effective and relevant. As the market continues to evolve, staying informed about regulatory changes and understanding their implications will be crucial for all participants in the cryptocurrency ecosystem.

Bearish Scenarios

In the ever-evolving world of cryptocurrencies, Bitcoin stands out as a revolutionary digital asset. However, it also faces significant challenges, particularly concerning its regulation and market integrity. As regulatory bodies worldwide grapple with the complexities of Bitcoin, it is crucial to understand the implications of these efforts and the delicate balance between innovation and oversight.

The global regulatory environment for Bitcoin is varied and constantly shifting. Different countries approach Bitcoin regulation with diverse strategies, reflecting their economic priorities, legal frameworks, and technological advancements. For instance, some nations have embraced Bitcoin, recognizing its potential to drive economic growth and financial inclusion. These countries have established clear regulatory frameworks that aim to foster innovation while ensuring consumer protection and market integrity. In contrast, other nations have taken a more cautious stance, implementing stringent regulations or outright bans to mitigate risks associated with money laundering, fraud, and market volatility.

Major regulatory bodies play pivotal roles in shaping the Bitcoin landscape. In the United States, the Securities and Exchange Commission (SEC) and the Commodity Futures Trading Commission (CFTC) are key players. The SEC focuses on ensuring that cryptocurrencies comply with securities laws, scrutinizing initial coin offerings (ICOs) and other investment vehicles to protect investors from fraud and market manipulation. The CFTC, on the other hand, oversees the trading of Bitcoin futures and derivatives, aiming to enhance transparency and reduce systemic risks in the market. Similarly, in Europe, the European Securities and Markets Authority (ESMA) and the European Central Bank (ECB) are instrumental in developing cohesive regulatory approaches across member states, fostering a unified market that balances innovation with consumer protection.

Recent regulatory developments highlight the dynamic nature of the Bitcoin market. In response to growing concerns about the environmental impact of Bitcoin mining, several countries have introduced regulations to promote sustainable practices. For example, some jurisdictions are incentivizing the use of renewable energy sources in mining operations, while others are considering carbon taxes to mitigate the ecological footprint of cryptocurrency activities. Additionally, the rise of decentralized finance (DeFi) platforms and non-fungible tokens (NFTs) has prompted regulators to expand their oversight, ensuring that these emerging sectors adhere to existing financial regulations and consumer protection standards.

One of the most significant challenges in regulating Bitcoin is balancing decentralization with the need for oversight. Bitcoin's decentralized nature, which is one of its core strengths, also poses unique regulatory challenges. Unlike traditional financial systems, Bitcoin operates without a central authority, making it difficult for regulators to enforce compliance and protect investors. This decentralized structure can sometimes facilitate illicit activities, such as money laundering and tax evasion, complicating regulatory efforts. Therefore, regulators must develop innovative approaches that respect the principles of decentralization while ensuring that the market remains transparent, secure, and fair.

Anonymity and privacy issues further complicate the regulatory landscape. While Bitcoin transactions are recorded on a public ledger, the identities of the parties involved are often pseudonymous. This feature, while enhancing user privacy, can also enable illegal activities and hinder law enforcement efforts. To address these concerns, regulators are increasingly focusing on Know Your Customer (KYC) and Anti-Money Laundering (AML) requirements. By mandating that cryptocurrency exchanges and other service providers verify the identities of their users, regulators aim to strike a balance between privacy and security, curbing illicit activities without compromising the fundamental principles of Bitcoin.

Jurisdictional conflicts present another layer of complexity in Bitcoin regulation. Given the global nature of cryptocurrencies, differing regulatory approaches across countries can create challenges for compliance and enforcement. For instance, a Bitcoin transaction may involve parties from multiple jurisdictions, each with its own set of rules and regulations. This fragmentation can lead to regulatory arbitrage, where market participants exploit inconsistencies between jurisdictions to circumvent regulations. To mitigate these issues, international cooperation and harmonization of regulatory standards are essential. Organizations such as the Financial Action Task Force (FATF) are working towards developing global standards for cryptocurrency regulation, promoting consistency and collaboration among countries.

Looking forward, potential regulatory models for Bitcoin must be flexible and adaptive to keep pace with technological advancements and market developments. Regulatory sandboxes, for example, provide a controlled environment for testing new technologies and business models under the supervision of regulators. This approach allows regulators to gain insights into the implications of emerging innovations while ensuring that consumer protection and market integrity are not compromised. Additionally, fostering dialogue between regulators, industry stakeholders, and the broader community is crucial for developing effective and inclusive regulatory frameworks.

The impact of regulation on the Bitcoin market is profound and multifaceted. On one hand, clear and consistent regulations can enhance market confidence, attracting institutional investors and promoting mainstream adoption. On the other hand, overly stringent regulations can stifle innovation and drive activities underground, exacerbating the very risks they aim to mitigate. Therefore, regulators must strive to achieve a delicate balance, creating an environment that encourages innovation while safeguarding the interests of all market participants.

In conclusion, the regulatory landscape for Bitcoin is complex and continually evolving. As regulators around the world navigate the challenges of overseeing a decentralized and rapidly changing market, their efforts will play a crucial role in shaping the future of Bitcoin. By understanding the intricacies of this regulatory environment, market participants can better navigate the landscape, making informed decisions that contribute to a more transparent, secure, and sustainable Bitcoin ecosystem.

Realistic Projections

In the evolving landscape of Bitcoin, understanding its complex market dynamics and the role of significant players is crucial. The presence of powerful market participants, often referred to as 'whales,' profoundly impacts Bitcoin's price movements. These whales, with their substantial Bitcoin holdings, have the ability to manipulate market prices to their advantage, creating an environment of extreme volatility. This volatility, while a hallmark of Bitcoin, raises critical questions about market integrity and the true value of Bitcoin as a decentralized financial asset.

Whales engage in various strategies to influence Bitcoin's price, exploiting their significant holdings to drive market trends. One common tactic is the "pump and dump" scheme, where the price of Bitcoin is artificially inflated through coordinated buying before being sold off at a peak, resulting in substantial profits for the manipulators while causing significant losses for unsuspecting investors. Another tactic is wash trading, where trades are made to create a false impression of market activity, misleading other traders about the true demand for Bitcoin. These manipulative practices distort the natural supply and demand dynamics of the market, making it challenging for retail investors to navigate the market effectively.

The impact of these manipulative tactics extends beyond individual losses, challenging the foundational principles of Bitcoin. The concentration of power in the hands of a few contradicts the decentralized ethos that Bitcoin was built upon. This centralization of influence can undermine trust in the cryptocurrency market, deterring new investors and stifling innovation. Furthermore, it highlights the need for regulatory measures to address these manipulative practices and foster a more transparent and stable market environment.

Despite these challenges, the Bitcoin market offers valuable lessons for traders and investors. Recognizing the signs of market manipulation and understanding the underlying dynamics can help market participants make more informed decisions. By staying vigilant and employing risk management strategies, traders can navigate the complexities of the Bitcoin market and mitigate potential losses. Moreover, the push for regulatory oversight and greater transparency can contribute to a healthier and more sustainable cryptocurrency ecosystem.

Bitcoin's paradox of being a revolutionary yet volatile asset underscores the complexities of its market dynamics. The interplay between its decentralized design and the manipulative practices of powerful market players creates a challenging environment for investors. As the cryptocurrency market continues to evolve, addressing these issues is crucial for realizing Bitcoin's original promise and ensuring its role in the future of finance.

This book aims to provide a comprehensive understanding of Bitcoin's unique position in the financial landscape, its inherent contradictions, and the mechanisms behind its unpredictable price movements. By shedding light on the forces that drive Bitcoin's volatility, this book seeks to educate and empower Bitcoin traders and investors, helping them recognize the signs of manipulation and make more informed decisions. Through meticulous research and analysis, it uncovers how market manipulators orchestrate massive price movements to their advantage, distorting the natural supply and demand dynamics of the Bitcoin market.

Moreover, the book addresses the broader implications of this manipulation for the future of Bitcoin and the cryptocurrency market as a whole. It raises critical questions about the sustainability of Bitcoin as a store of value and its potential to fulfill its original promise of a decentralized, fair financial system. By exploring potential solutions and regulatory measures, it aims to foster a more transparent and stable market environment, ultimately contributing to a healthier and more sustainable cryptocurrency ecosystem.

In essence, this book is a wake-up call to the Bitcoin community and beyond. It challenges the prevailing narratives about Bitcoin's price volatility and exposes the hidden forces at play. Whether you are a seasoned trader, a new investor, or simply curious about the world of cryptocurrencies, this book offers invaluable insights into the complexities of the Bitcoin market and the urgent need for greater transparency and fairness.

Innovations and Technological Advances

Layer 2 Solutions

In the evolving landscape of Bitcoin, Layer 2 solutions have emerged as crucial innovations aimed at addressing the scalability and transaction speed issues inherent in the original blockchain. Bitcoin, while revolutionary, faces significant challenges due to its design limitations, which can lead to slow transaction times and high fees during periods of high demand. Layer 2 solutions are designed to mitigate these problems by enabling transactions to occur off the main Bitcoin blockchain, thus increasing efficiency and reducing congestion.

One of the most prominent Layer 2 solutions is the Lightning Network. This technology allows for the creation of payment channels between parties, facilitating transactions that are both instant and low-cost. By conducting multiple transactions off-chain and then recording the net result on the main blockchain, the Lightning Network alleviates the load on the primary network, enhancing its capacity to handle a higher volume of transactions.

The concept behind the Lightning Network revolves around the establishment of bi-directional payment channels. Once these channels are set up, users can transact with each other without the need to broadcast every single transaction to the Bitcoin blockchain. This not only speeds up the transaction process but also significantly reduces the transaction fees, making microtransactions feasible. The final state of the transactions is later recorded on the blockchain, ensuring security and integrity while maintaining efficiency.

Another notable Layer 2 solution is the Liquid Network, which is designed to facilitate fast and secure transfers of Bitcoin between exchanges. The Liquid Network uses a sidechain, which is a separate blockchain pegged to Bitcoin, to allow for quicker transactions with enhanced privacy features. This is particularly beneficial for traders and exchanges, as it enables them to move large amounts of Bitcoin rapidly and confidentially, without waiting for multiple confirmations on the main blockchain.

The implementation of these Layer 2 solutions is not without its challenges. The adoption of the Lightning Network, for instance, requires users to lock up a portion of their Bitcoin in payment channels, which can be seen as a barrier to entry. Additionally, the security of off-chain transactions and the potential for network centralization remain concerns that need to be addressed. However, continuous development and increasing user adoption are gradually overcoming these hurdles.

Furthermore, Layer 2 solutions like the Lightning Network and the Liquid Network represent significant steps forward in the quest to scale Bitcoin. They exemplify how innovative technologies can address the limitations of existing blockchain infrastructures, paving the way for Bitcoin to function more effectively as a global currency.

In conclusion, Layer 2 solutions are vital to the future of Bitcoin. They provide a means to overcome the inherent scalability issues, enabling faster and cheaper transactions. As these technologies evolve and become more widely adopted, they will play a crucial role in realizing Bitcoin's potential as a decentralized and efficient medium of exchange.

Integrating with Traditional Finance

In exploring the potential for Bitcoin to integrate with traditional financial systems, it is essential to understand both the challenges and opportunities presented by this convergence. Traditional finance operates on principles and infrastructures developed over centuries, ensuring stability, security, and regulatory compliance. In contrast, Bitcoin represents a decentralized, innovative, and often disruptive technology. Integrating these two realms requires addressing several key aspects: interoperability, regulatory frameworks, and the mutual benefits for both systems.

One of the primary challenges in integrating Bitcoin with traditional finance is interoperability. Traditional financial systems rely on centralized databases and trusted intermediaries, whereas Bitcoin operates on a decentralized ledger without intermediaries. Bridging this gap involves developing technological solutions that allow seamless transactions between these fundamentally different systems. Initiatives such as atomic swaps, which enable direct exchange of cryptocurrencies for traditional assets without intermediaries, and the development of robust APIs (Application Programming Interfaces) are steps towards achieving this interoperability.

Regulatory frameworks pose another significant challenge. Traditional finance is heavily regulated to protect consumers, maintain market integrity, and prevent illicit activities such as money laundering and fraud. Bitcoin, being decentralized and pseudonymous, presents unique regulatory challenges. Financial institutions seeking to integrate Bitcoin must navigate a complex landscape of regulations that vary widely across jurisdictions. This requires a concerted effort to develop compliance solutions that adhere to existing regulations while accommodating the unique aspects of Bitcoin. Regulatory clarity and the development of global standards are crucial for facilitating integration and fostering innovation.

Despite these challenges, the integration of Bitcoin with traditional finance offers numerous benefits. For traditional financial institutions, embracing Bitcoin can provide access to a new asset class, attract tech-savvy clients, and enhance their offerings with blockchain-based solutions such as faster and more secure cross-border transactions. For Bitcoin, integration with traditional finance can provide greater legitimacy, increased liquidity, and broader acceptance as a viable financial instrument. Collaborative efforts between fintech companies and traditional financial institutions are already paving the way for innovative solutions that leverage the strengths of both systems.

Moreover, the integration of Bitcoin with traditional finance can drive financial inclusion. In many parts of the world, access to traditional banking services is limited. Bitcoin, with its decentralized nature, offers an alternative means of financial inclusion. By integrating Bitcoin into their services, financial institutions can reach underserved populations, providing them with access to financial services and fostering economic growth.

In conclusion, the integration of Bitcoin with traditional finance is a complex but promising endeavor. It requires addressing technological interoperability, navigating regulatory challenges, and leveraging the mutual benefits for both systems. As this integration progresses, it has the potential to transform the financial landscape, offering innovative solutions, enhancing financial inclusion, and driving the adoption of decentralized technologies in mainstream finance.

Emerging Technologies

Bitcoin, often heralded as the pioneering cryptocurrency, promised a revolutionary alternative to traditional financial systems. Its decentralized design, transparent nature, and the fixed supply cap of 21 million units suggested a secure and stable asset. However, the reality of Bitcoin's market behavior starkly contrasts with these expectations, as it is notorious for its extreme volatility. This paradox raises critical questions about the factors driving such fluctuations and the integrity of the market itself.

Bitcoin was envisioned as a response to the flaws of centralized financial systems. Its blockchain technology ensures that every transaction is recorded on a public ledger, accessible to anyone and immutable once confirmed. This transparency and security were intended to eliminate the need for intermediaries, reduce transaction costs, and provide a democratized financial ecosystem. The fixed supply cap was designed to protect against inflation, a common issue with fiat currencies that can be printed at will by central banks. In theory, these attributes should create a stable and appreciating value as demand for Bitcoin increases.

However, Bitcoin's market behavior reveals a different story. The price of Bitcoin has been subject to extreme volatility, influenced by speculation and market manipulation. Significant price fluctuations are often attributed to the activities of large holders, known as "whales," who can influence the market with their substantial holdings. These whales, by owning a large portion of the Bitcoin supply, have the power to manipulate prices through coordinated buying and selling, creating artificial highs and lows to maximize their profits. This manipulation distorts the natural supply and demand dynamics, leading to unpredictable market movements that can result in significant losses for unsuspecting traders.

The tools and strategies employed by these manipulators are sophisticated and multifaceted. Techniques such as wash trading, where an investor simultaneously buys and sells the same financial instruments to create misleading market activity, and pump and dump schemes, where the price of an asset is artificially inflated to attract investors before being sold off at a profit, are commonly used. These tactics create an illusion of market sentiment, driving irrational behavior among traders and exacerbating volatility. The impact of such manipulation is profound, undermining the foundational principles of Bitcoin and raising questions about its sustainability as a store of value.

The broader implications of this market manipulation extend beyond individual losses. They challenge the very essence of Bitcoin's promise as a decentralized and fair financial system. The concentration of power in the hands of a few large players contradicts the ideals of decentralization and democratization that Bitcoin was supposed to represent. This centralization of influence can erode trust in the cryptocurrency market, deterring new investors and stifling innovation. Furthermore, it highlights the urgent need for regulatory measures to address these manipulative practices and foster a more transparent and stable market environment.

While Bitcoin's volatility and susceptibility to manipulation present significant challenges, they also offer valuable lessons for traders and investors. Recognizing the signs of market manipulation and understanding the underlying dynamics can help market participants make more informed decisions. By staying vigilant and employing risk management strategies, traders can navigate the complexities of the Bitcoin market and mitigate potential losses. Moreover, the push for regulatory oversight and greater transparency can contribute to a healthier and more sustainable cryptocurrency ecosystem.

Bitcoin's paradox of being a revolutionary yet volatile asset underscores the complexities of its market dynamics. The interplay between its decentralized design and the manipulative practices of powerful market players creates a challenging environment for investors. As the cryptocurrency market continues to evolve, addressing these issues is crucial for realizing Bitcoin's original promise and ensuring its role in the future of finance.

The promise of Bitcoin, its early optimism, and the subsequent market reality paint a complex picture of an asset that was supposed to revolutionize finance but instead became a hotbed for speculation and manipulation. This discrepancy between expectation and reality underscores the need for a deeper understanding and more robust regulatory frameworks to protect the market's integrity. As the market matures, learning from these lessons and adapting to the challenges presented will be essential for Bitcoin to fulfill its revolutionary potential.

Bitcoin in the Global Economy

Bitcoin as Legal Tender

Understanding the intricacies of Bitcoin as a legal tender reveals a complex interplay of technological, economic, and regulatory factors. When El Salvador became the first country to adopt Bitcoin as legal tender in September 2021, it marked a significant milestone in the cryptocurrency's evolution. This move highlighted both the potential benefits and challenges associated with integrating Bitcoin into a nation's financial system.

Bitcoin's decentralized nature and blockchain technology offer several advantages when used as legal tender. One of the primary benefits is the enhancement of financial inclusion. In many developing countries, a significant portion of the population remains unbanked, lacking access to traditional financial services. Bitcoin, with its ability to be transferred and stored on a smartphone, presents an accessible alternative for these populations. This digital currency can facilitate remittances, which are crucial for many economies, by reducing transaction costs and increasing the speed of cross-border transfers.

However, adopting Bitcoin as legal tender also presents several challenges. One of the most prominent issues is the extreme volatility of Bitcoin's price. Unlike traditional currencies, which are generally stable and influenced by monetary policy, Bitcoin's value can fluctuate wildly within short periods. This volatility can undermine its effectiveness as a stable medium of exchange and store of value. For businesses and consumers, such fluctuations can pose significant risks, making financial planning and pricing difficult.

Regulatory and infrastructural challenges also come into play. Integrating Bitcoin into a country's financial system requires substantial investment in technology and education. Merchants need the necessary infrastructure to accept Bitcoin payments, and consumers must be educated on how to use and secure their Bitcoin holdings. Additionally, governments must develop regulatory frameworks to address issues such as taxation, anti-money laundering (AML), and combating the financing of terrorism (CFT). These frameworks must balance encouraging innovation and protecting consumers and the financial system's integrity.

Moreover, the use of Bitcoin as legal tender raises questions about monetary sovereignty. Traditionally, national currencies have been under the control of central banks, which manage monetary policy to influence inflation, employment, and economic growth. Bitcoin, being decentralized and not controlled by any single entity, challenges this traditional model. For countries like El Salvador, which do not have their currency and use the US dollar, adopting Bitcoin can be seen as an attempt to gain more control over monetary policy. However, it also means relinquishing control over the money supply to a decentralized network.

The international response to Bitcoin's adoption as legal tender has been mixed. While some view it as a bold and innovative step, others, including international financial institutions, have expressed concerns. The International Monetary Fund (IMF), for instance, has warned about the potential risks to financial stability and consumer protection. These concerns highlight the need for careful consideration and planning when integrating Bitcoin into a nation's financial system.

In conclusion, the adoption of Bitcoin as legal tender is a multifaceted issue that involves balancing potential benefits with significant challenges. While it can enhance financial inclusion and reduce transaction costs, its volatility, regulatory requirements, and implications for monetary sovereignty must be carefully managed. As more countries consider similar moves, the lessons learned from early adopters like El Salvador will be crucial in shaping the future of Bitcoin and other cryptocurrencies in the global economy.

Bitcoin's Role in Financial Inclusion

In exploring the potential for Bitcoin to integrate with traditional finance, it is essential to consider the broader landscape of emerging technologies and how they intersect with established financial systems. The convergence of Bitcoin and traditional finance is not just about the adoption of a new form of currency but involves a comprehensive overhaul of financial infrastructures, regulatory frameworks, and market practices.

Layer 2 solutions, such as the Lightning Network, play a critical role in enhancing Bitcoin's scalability and transaction speed. These solutions facilitate microtransactions and improve the overall efficiency of the Bitcoin network. However, for Bitcoin to seamlessly integrate with traditional finance, more sophisticated and robust infrastructures are required. This includes secure and reliable custodial services, interoperability protocols, and compliance mechanisms that align with global financial standards.

The traditional financial sector operates under stringent regulatory oversight, ensuring transparency, security, and consumer protection. Bitcoin, in its essence, challenges these norms with its decentralized and pseudonymous nature. Therefore, integrating Bitcoin into traditional finance demands a harmonization of regulatory requirements without compromising the core principles of Bitcoin. This involves creating regulatory sandboxes, where new technologies can be tested under a controlled environment, and developing frameworks that recognize and address the unique characteristics of digital assets.

Institutional adoption of Bitcoin is a significant step towards integration with traditional finance. Large financial institutions, such as banks, hedge funds, and investment firms, have started to recognize Bitcoin as a viable asset class. This shift is driven by the growing demand for digital assets among investors and the increasing realization of Bitcoin's potential as a hedge against inflation and currency devaluation. To support this adoption, financial institutions are developing new financial products, such as Bitcoin ETFs, futures, and options, which provide traditional investors with exposure to Bitcoin without the need to directly hold the asset.

Furthermore, the rise of decentralized finance (DeFi) platforms represents another critical intersection of Bitcoin and traditional finance. DeFi leverages blockchain technology to offer financial services, such as lending, borrowing, and trading, in a decentralized manner. By integrating Bitcoin into DeFi ecosystems, users can utilize Bitcoin as collateral for loans, earn interest on their Bitcoin holdings, and engage in decentralized trading. This integration not only enhances the utility of Bitcoin but also bridges the gap between traditional and decentralized financial systems.

However, the integration of Bitcoin with traditional finance is not without challenges. One of the primary concerns is the volatility of Bitcoin, which can pose significant risks to financial stability. Traditional financial institutions are accustomed to dealing with relatively stable asset classes, and the extreme price fluctuations of Bitcoin require the development of new risk management strategies. Additionally, the regulatory landscape for Bitcoin and other digital assets is still evolving, creating uncertainty and potential legal hurdles for institutions seeking to integrate Bitcoin into their operations.

Another critical aspect is the technological integration. Traditional financial systems are built on legacy technologies that may not be compatible with blockchain-based solutions. Ensuring interoperability between these systems requires significant investment in technology upgrades and the development of new interoperability standards. Additionally, cybersecurity is a paramount concern, as the integration of Bitcoin into traditional finance increases the attack surface for cyber threats.

In conclusion, integrating Bitcoin with traditional finance involves a multifaceted approach that addresses regulatory, technological, and market challenges. By leveraging emerging technologies, such as Layer 2 solutions and DeFi, and developing robust regulatory frameworks, the financial sector can harness the potential of Bitcoin while maintaining stability and security. This integration not only enhances the utility of Bitcoin but also paves the way for a more inclusive and innovative financial system. As the landscape continues to evolve, ongoing collaboration between regulators, financial institutions, and technology developers will be crucial in realizing the full potential of Bitcoin in traditional finance.

Bitcoin and Geopolitics

Bitcoin's rise as a global financial phenomenon has not only influenced individual investors and markets but has also attracted significant attention from governments and geopolitical entities worldwide. Its decentralized nature and the potential to operate outside traditional financial systems present both opportunities and challenges that transcend borders. This unique positioning of Bitcoin has led to its involvement in various geopolitical strategies and conflicts, making it a subject of intense scrutiny and debate.

One of the primary geopolitical dimensions of Bitcoin is its potential to serve as a tool for financial sovereignty. In countries facing economic sanctions or financial instability, Bitcoin offers an alternative means of conducting transactions and storing value, independent of government-controlled financial systems. For instance, in nations like Venezuela and Iran, where access to global financial markets is restricted due to sanctions, Bitcoin has emerged as a viable option for circumventing these economic barriers. This ability to operate outside conventional financial constraints has significant implications for international relations and economic policies.

Moreover, Bitcoin's role in facilitating financial inclusion has geopolitical ramifications. In regions with underdeveloped banking infrastructure, Bitcoin and other cryptocurrencies can provide access to financial services for the unbanked population. This potential for financial empowerment can shift economic dynamics, fostering development and reducing dependency on traditional financial institutions. As a result, governments in these regions are increasingly interested in the regulatory and infrastructural aspects of Bitcoin adoption, recognizing its potential to drive economic growth and stability.

However, the decentralized and pseudonymous nature of Bitcoin also poses significant challenges to global security and regulatory frameworks. The use of Bitcoin in illicit activities, such as money laundering, terrorist financing, and cybercrime, has raised concerns among international regulatory bodies. Governments worldwide are grappling with the task of integrating

Bitcoin into their financial systems while mitigating the risks associated with its misuse. This has led to a complex landscape of regulatory responses, ranging from outright bans to the development of comprehensive regulatory frameworks aimed at ensuring transparency and accountability.

In addition to regulatory challenges, Bitcoin's impact on global financial stability is a critical concern for policymakers. The significant price volatility and speculative nature of Bitcoin can lead to financial instability, particularly in emerging markets with less resilient financial systems. The interconnectedness of global financial markets means that extreme fluctuations in Bitcoin's value can have ripple effects, influencing investor behavior and market dynamics across the world. As such, international financial institutions and governments are closely monitoring Bitcoin's market behavior and its potential implications for global economic stability.

Furthermore, Bitcoin's influence extends to the realm of international trade and monetary policy. As more businesses and individuals adopt Bitcoin for transactions, there is a growing discourse on its potential to function as a global reserve currency. This possibility challenges the traditional dominance of fiat currencies, particularly the US dollar, in international trade and finance. The prospect of a decentralized digital currency gaining prominence on the global stage introduces new dynamics in monetary policy and international economic relations.

In conclusion, Bitcoin's intersection with geopolitics is multifaceted and complex, encompassing issues of financial sovereignty, regulatory challenges, global security, and economic stability. Its decentralized nature and global reach make it a powerful tool for both empowerment and disruption. As governments and international bodies navigate the evolving landscape of cryptocurrency, the geopolitical implications of Bitcoin will continue to be a critical area of focus, shaping the future of global finance and economic policies. The ongoing dialogue between innovation and regulation will determine how

Bitcoin integrates into the broader geopolitical context, influencing the balance of power and economic dynamics in the years to come.

Chapter 7: Protecting Yourself in the Bitcoin Market

Risk Management Strategies

Diversification

In considering the potential scenarios for Bitcoin's future, the integration with traditional finance remains a pivotal area of exploration. This dynamic is not merely a technological challenge but one that encompasses regulatory, strategic, and economic dimensions. Traditional financial institutions and mechanisms operate on a foundation of established protocols and trust systems that have evolved over centuries. Integrating Bitcoin, a decentralized and relatively new financial asset, into this traditional ecosystem presents both opportunities and challenges.

The journey of integrating Bitcoin into traditional finance began with the recognition of Bitcoin as a legitimate asset class. Initially viewed with skepticism, Bitcoin has gradually garnered acceptance among mainstream financial entities. This acceptance is marked by several key milestones, such as major financial institutions offering Bitcoin-related services, the introduction of Bitcoin futures and exchange-traded funds (ETFs), and the entry of Bitcoin into the balance sheets of publicly traded companies. These developments signify a growing convergence between traditional finance and digital currencies, fostering an environment where Bitcoin can be utilized within existing financial frameworks.

One of the most profound impacts of integrating Bitcoin with traditional finance is the potential for increased liquidity and market stability. Traditional financial markets are characterized by deep liquidity pools and robust trading infrastructures that mitigate extreme volatility. By integrating Bitcoin into these markets, the cryptocurrency can benefit from enhanced liquidity, reducing the drastic price swings that have historically plagued it. Additionally, the participation of institutional investors, who typically engage in more sophisticated and long-term investment strategies, can further stabilize Bitcoin's price and foster a more mature market environment.

However, this integration is not without its challenges. Regulatory compliance remains a significant hurdle. Traditional financial institutions operate under stringent regulatory frameworks designed to ensure market integrity, protect investors, and prevent illicit activities. Bitcoin, with its decentralized and pseudonymous nature, poses unique regulatory challenges. Governments and regulatory bodies around the world are grappling with how to effectively regulate Bitcoin without stifling innovation. Striking a balance between fostering the growth of digital currencies and ensuring regulatory compliance is crucial for the seamless integration of Bitcoin into traditional finance.

Another critical aspect of this integration is the technological compatibility between traditional financial systems and blockchain technology. Traditional financial systems are built on legacy infrastructure that may not easily interface with blockchain's decentralized and distributed ledger technology. Bridging this technological gap requires significant investment in innovation and infrastructure. Financial institutions are increasingly exploring blockchain technology to enhance their operations, with initiatives such as blockchain-based settlement systems and digital asset custody solutions. These advancements are paving the way for a more integrated financial ecosystem where Bitcoin and other digital assets can coexist with traditional financial instruments.

Furthermore, the integration of Bitcoin into traditional finance also opens up new avenues for financial inclusion. Traditional banking systems often exclude individuals and communities in remote or underbanked regions due to the high costs of infrastructure and regulatory compliance. Bitcoin, with its borderless and decentralized nature, offers an alternative that can reach these underserved populations. By integrating Bitcoin into traditional finance, financial institutions can leverage the strengths of both systems to offer more inclusive financial services, thereby bridging the gap between the unbanked and the global financial system.

In conclusion, the integration of Bitcoin with traditional finance is a multifaceted process that holds the promise of increased liquidity, market stability, and financial inclusion. However, it also presents significant challenges, particularly in the realms of regulatory compliance and technological compatibility. As the financial landscape continues to evolve, the successful integration of Bitcoin into traditional finance will depend on collaborative efforts between regulators, financial institutions, and the cryptocurrency community. This convergence has the potential to redefine the future of finance, creating a more inclusive and resilient financial ecosystem that harnesses the strengths of both traditional and digital currencies.

Stop Loss and Take Profit

In the evolving landscape of digital currencies, Bitcoin stands out as a revolutionary asset with the potential to redefine traditional financial systems. Its promise of decentralization, transparency, and a fixed supply cap has captivated the imagination of investors and technologists alike. However, the reality of Bitcoin's market behavior often diverges from these ideals, particularly when considering the influence of market participants and the impact of their strategies.

Bitcoin, by design, is capped at 21 million coins, a feature intended to protect against inflation and ensure a stable store of value. Despite this, Bitcoin's market is notorious for its extreme volatility, with prices subject to dramatic fluctuations. This volatility can be attributed to the activities of key market participants, commonly referred to as "whales," who hold a significant portion of the Bitcoin supply. These individuals and entities possess the power to manipulate market prices through their substantial holdings, creating artificial highs and lows to maximize their profits.

The concept of "whales" in the Bitcoin market refers to large holders who can influence price movements through coordinated buying and selling strategies. Their actions often distort the natural supply and demand dynamics, leading to unpredictable market conditions. This manipulation is facilitated by various tactics, including wash trading and pump and dump schemes, which create misleading market activity and sentiment. The impact of such practices extends beyond individual losses, challenging the foundational principles of Bitcoin and raising questions about its sustainability as a decentralized financial system.

Wash trading involves an investor simultaneously buying and selling the same financial instruments to create the illusion of market activity. This tactic misleads other market participants, driving irrational behavior and exacerbating volatility. Similarly, pump and dump schemes artificially inflate the price of an asset to attract investors, only for the manipulators to sell off their holdings at a profit, leaving others with significant losses. These deceptive practices undermine market integrity and erode trust in the cryptocurrency ecosystem.

The concentration of Bitcoin ownership among a few large holders contradicts the decentralized ideals that underpin the cryptocurrency. This centralization of influence can deter new investors and stifle innovation, highlighting the need for regulatory measures to address manipulative practices and foster a more transparent and stable market environment. Recognizing the signs of market manipulation and understanding the underlying dynamics are crucial for traders and investors to make informed decisions and mitigate potential losses.

Moreover, the broader implications of Bitcoin's volatility and susceptibility to manipulation extend to its role in the global economy. Bitcoin's promise as a decentralized and fair financial system is compromised by the actions of powerful market players. The need for greater regulatory oversight and transparency is critical to ensuring a healthier and more sustainable cryptocurrency market. By addressing these challenges, Bitcoin can better fulfill its potential as a transformative asset in the financial landscape.

As the cryptocurrency market continues to evolve, the interplay between Bitcoin's decentralized design and the manipulative practices of market participants will remain a focal point for regulators, traders, and investors. Addressing these issues is essential for realizing Bitcoin's original promise and ensuring its role in the future of finance. Through vigilance, education, and regulatory intervention, the cryptocurrency ecosystem can move towards greater transparency and fairness, fostering a more stable and inclusive financial environment.

Staying Informed

Bitcoin, the pioneering cryptocurrency, was introduced with the promise of revolutionizing the financial system. Its design as a decentralized and transparent form of digital currency seemed to offer a secure and stable alternative to traditional financial systems. Bitcoin's decentralized nature, underpinned by blockchain technology, and its finite supply cap of 21 million units suggested that it would function as a stable and appreciating asset. However, the reality of Bitcoin's market behavior starkly contrasts with these expectations. Instead of stability, Bitcoin is notorious for its extreme volatility, with prices swinging wildly within short periods. This paradox raises critical questions about the factors driving such fluctuations and the integrity of the market itself.

At its core, Bitcoin was envisioned as a response to the flaws of centralized financial systems. Its blockchain technology ensures that every transaction is recorded on a public ledger, accessible to anyone and immutable once confirmed. This transparency and security were intended to eliminate the need for intermediaries, reduce transaction costs, and provide a democratized financial ecosystem. The fixed supply cap of 21 million Bitcoins was designed to protect against inflation, a common issue with fiat currencies that can be printed at will by central banks. In theory, these attributes should create a stable and appreciating value as demand for Bitcoin increases.

However, Bitcoin's market behavior reveals a different story. The price of Bitcoin has been subject to extreme volatility, influenced by speculation and market manipulation. The significant price fluctuations are often attributed to the activities of large holders, known as "whales," who can influence the market with their substantial holdings. These whales, by owning a large portion of the Bitcoin supply, have the power to manipulate prices through coordinated buying and selling, creating artificial highs and lows to maximize their profits. This manipulation distorts the natural supply and demand dynamics, leading to unpredictable market movements that can result in significant losses for unsuspecting traders.

The tools and strategies employed by these manipulators are sophisticated and multifaceted. Techniques such as wash trading, where an investor simultaneously buys and sells the same financial instruments to create misleading market activity, and pump and dump schemes, where the price of an asset is artificially inflated to attract investors before being sold off at a profit, are commonly used. These tactics create an illusion of market sentiment, driving irrational behavior among traders and exacerbating volatility. The impact of such manipulation is profound, undermining the foundational principles of Bitcoin and raising questions about its sustainability as a store of value.

The broader implications of this market manipulation extend beyond individual losses. They challenge the very essence of Bitcoin's promise as a decentralized and fair financial system. The concentration of power in the hands of a few large players contradicts the ideals of decentralization and democratization that Bitcoin was supposed to represent. This centralization of influence can erode trust in the cryptocurrency market, deterring new investors and stifling innovation. Furthermore, it highlights the urgent need for regulatory measures to address these manipulative practices and foster a more transparent and stable market environment.

While Bitcoin's volatility and susceptibility to manipulation present significant challenges, they also offer valuable lessons for traders and investors. Recognizing the signs of market manipulation and understanding the underlying dynamics can help market participants make more informed decisions. By staying vigilant and employing risk management strategies, traders can navigate the complexities of the Bitcoin market and mitigate potential losses. Moreover, the push for regulatory oversight and greater transparency can contribute to a healthier and more sustainable cryptocurrency ecosystem.

Bitcoin's paradox of being a revolutionary yet volatile asset underscores the complexities of its market dynamics. The interplay between its decentralized design and the manipulative practices of powerful market players creates a challenging environment for investors. As the cryptocurrency market continues to evolve, addressing these issues is crucial for realizing Bitcoin's original promise and ensuring its role in the future of finance.

Understanding these dynamics becomes even more crucial when considering the intricate relationship between Bitcoin and geopolitics. Bitcoin operates on a global scale, transcending national borders and traditional financial systems. This global nature poses unique challenges and opportunities, particularly in how different countries approach regulation and integration of cryptocurrencies. Geopolitical events can significantly impact Bitcoin's price and adoption, as seen in various instances where governmental actions or political instability have led to substantial market reactions.

Countries with more progressive regulatory frameworks and technological infrastructure may see higher adoption rates, while those with restrictive policies may hinder Bitcoin's growth. The decentralized nature of Bitcoin means that it can be used as a tool for financial inclusion, especially in regions with unstable financial systems. However, this also means that it can be used to circumvent traditional financial regulations, raising concerns about its use in illegal activities.

The tension between decentralization and regulation is a central theme in the ongoing evolution of Bitcoin. While its decentralized nature provides resilience and security, the lack of regulatory oversight can lead to exploitation and market manipulation. Finding a balance between maintaining the decentralized ethos of Bitcoin while implementing effective regulatory measures is critical for its long-term viability.

In conclusion, the future of Bitcoin will be shaped by how it navigates these challenges. Its success will depend on addressing the paradoxes and contradictions within its design and market behavior. As Bitcoin continues to mature, it will need to adapt to the evolving landscape of global finance, balancing the need for security, transparency, and decentralization with the realities of market manipulation and regulatory scrutiny. The insights gained from understanding Bitcoin's current dynamics can pave the way for a more robust and equitable financial system in the future.

Recognizing Manipulative Patterns

Identifying Red Flags

Identifying red flags in the Bitcoin market is crucial for both novice and experienced investors. Understanding these warning signs can prevent substantial financial losses and ensure a more informed trading strategy. Several indicators can serve as red flags, signaling potential market manipulation or impending price shifts that traders should be aware of.

One of the primary red flags is sudden and unexplained price movements. If Bitcoin's price experiences a sharp increase or decrease without any significant news or events to justify the change, it could indicate market manipulation. Whales, or large holders of Bitcoin, often orchestrate these movements to create a buying or selling frenzy, which they can exploit for profit. Traders should be wary of such movements and investigate the underlying causes before making any trading decisions.

Another red flag is unusual trading volume. A sudden spike in trading volume can indicate that large players are entering or exiting the market. This activity can precede significant price changes and may be part of a larger strategy to manipulate the market. Monitoring trading volume alongside price movements can provide insights into the market's true sentiment and help identify potential manipulation.

Additionally, the presence of large buy or sell orders in the order book can be a warning sign. These large orders, often placed by whales, can create a psychological effect on other traders, prompting them to buy or sell based on the perceived demand or supply. This tactic, known as spoofing, can distort the market and lead to irrational trading behaviors. Traders should be cautious when they observe these large orders and consider the possibility of manipulation.

Social media and news can also play a significant role in influencing Bitcoin's price. Sudden surges in positive or negative news about Bitcoin can trigger price movements. However, not all news is genuine; some may be part of a coordinated effort to manipulate the market. Traders should critically evaluate the sources of news and cross-reference information before making any trading decisions.

Technical analysis can also reveal red flags. Patterns such as head and shoulders, double tops, or bottoms, and other reversal patterns can indicate potential price reversals. However, these patterns can also be manipulated by large players to create false signals. Traders should use technical analysis in conjunction with other indicators and remain cautious of relying solely on chart patterns.

Finally, regulatory news and developments can impact Bitcoin's price. Sudden announcements of regulatory crackdowns or support for cryptocurrencies can cause significant price movements. Keeping abreast of regulatory changes and understanding their potential impact on the market is essential for identifying potential red flags.

In conclusion, identifying red flags in the Bitcoin market requires vigilance and a multifaceted approach. By monitoring price movements, trading volume, order book activity, news, and technical indicators, traders can better understand the market's underlying dynamics and avoid potential pitfalls. Staying informed and critically evaluating market signals can help traders navigate the complexities of the Bitcoin market and protect their investments from manipulation and sudden shifts.

Analyzing Market Sentiment

The global regulatory environment for Bitcoin is both complex and fragmented, reflecting the diverse attitudes and approaches of different nations towards cryptocurrency. As Bitcoin gained popularity, governments and regulatory bodies worldwide have struggled to develop frameworks that address its unique characteristics while mitigating associated risks. The regulatory landscape continues to evolve, influenced by Bitcoin's impact on traditional financial systems, its potential for innovation, and concerns about illegal activities.

In countries like the United States, the regulatory approach to Bitcoin has been multifaceted. Various agencies such as the Securities and Exchange Commission (SEC), the Commodity Futures Trading Commission (CFTC), and the Financial Crimes Enforcement Network (FinCEN) have asserted their jurisdiction over different aspects of Bitcoin and other cryptocurrencies. The SEC has focused on regulating Initial Coin Offerings (ICOs) and determining whether specific digital assets should be classified as securities. The CFTC has oversight over Bitcoin futures and other derivatives, while FinCEN monitors anti-money laundering (AML) and counter-terrorism financing (CTF) compliance.

In contrast, the European Union has sought to harmonize cryptocurrency regulation across its member states through comprehensive legislation like the Markets in Crypto-Assets (MiCA) regulation. MiCA aims to create a clear legal framework for digital assets, ensuring consumer protection and market integrity while fostering innovation. This regulation is designed to address the challenges posed by the rapid growth of cryptocurrencies and to prevent regulatory arbitrage within the EU.

Asia presents a varied regulatory landscape, with countries like Japan adopting a progressive stance towards Bitcoin. Japan was one of the first countries to recognize Bitcoin as legal tender, implementing robust regulatory measures to oversee exchanges and protect consumers. The Financial Services Agency (FSA) enforces stringent requirements for registration, compliance, and security, making Japan a model for cryptocurrency regulation.

Conversely, China has taken a more restrictive approach, banning cryptocurrency exchanges and ICOs while promoting its own digital currency, the Digital Yuan. The Chinese government cites concerns over financial stability, fraud, and capital flight as reasons for its stringent measures. However, China remains a significant player in the Bitcoin mining industry, which presents a paradox in its regulatory stance.

In emerging markets, countries like Nigeria and El Salvador illustrate diverse regulatory approaches. Nigeria, despite having one of the highest rates of Bitcoin adoption, has seen its central bank impose restrictions on cryptocurrency transactions within the banking sector. In contrast, El Salvador made history by becoming the first country to adopt Bitcoin as legal tender, aiming to enhance financial inclusion and attract foreign investment. This bold move has drawn global attention and scrutiny, highlighting the potential benefits and challenges of integrating Bitcoin into a national economy.

International organizations such as the Financial Action Task Force (FATF) play a crucial role in shaping the global regulatory environment for Bitcoin. The FATF sets standards and promotes the effective implementation of legal, regulatory, and operational measures to combat money laundering, terrorist financing, and other related threats. Its guidelines on cryptocurrency aim to ensure that countries adopt a coordinated approach to regulation, addressing risks while allowing for innovation.

The global regulatory environment for Bitcoin is continually evolving as regulators balance the need to protect consumers and ensure market integrity with the desire to foster innovation and economic growth. As Bitcoin continues to gain mainstream acceptance, the development of coherent and effective regulatory frameworks will be essential in shaping its future role in the global financial system.

Protecting Against FOMO and FUD

Bitcoin's potential to promote financial inclusion is a widely discussed topic, given its decentralized nature and accessibility. As a digital currency, Bitcoin provides an opportunity for individuals in underserved or unbanked regions to participate in the global economy. Traditional banking systems often exclude large portions of the population due to lack of infrastructure, documentation, or financial literacy. Bitcoin, however, requires only internet access and a digital wallet, which can be set up with minimal barriers, thus offering an inclusive financial alternative.

One of the most significant advantages of Bitcoin is its ability to facilitate peer-to-peer transactions without the need for intermediaries such as banks or payment processors. This feature is particularly beneficial for people in developing countries where banking services are limited or non-existent. By enabling direct transactions, Bitcoin reduces transaction costs and increases efficiency, allowing users to transfer funds quickly and securely across borders. This capability is crucial for remittances, which are a vital source of income for many families in developing nations. Traditional remittance services often charge high fees and take several days to process transactions, but Bitcoin can significantly reduce these costs and timeframes, making more funds available to recipients.

Furthermore, Bitcoin can act as a hedge against local currency devaluation and economic instability. In countries with high inflation rates or unstable financial systems, individuals often seek alternatives to protect their wealth. Bitcoin, with its fixed supply and decentralized nature, offers a potential store of value that is not subject to the same risks as local currencies. This attribute can provide financial security and stability to individuals living in volatile economic environments.

Bitcoin's role in financial inclusion extends beyond individual users to small and medium-sized enterprises (SMEs). SMEs in developing regions often face challenges in accessing traditional financial services, such as obtaining loans or opening business accounts. Bitcoin can provide these businesses with access to a broader range of financial services, including crowdfunding and microloans facilitated through blockchain technology. This access can help SMEs grow and expand, contributing to local economic development.

Educational initiatives and technological advancements also play a crucial role in enhancing Bitcoin's impact on financial inclusion. Increasing awareness and understanding of Bitcoin and blockchain technology can empower more people to take advantage of its benefits. Additionally, the development of user-friendly platforms and applications can make Bitcoin more accessible to those with limited technological expertise.

However, it is essential to acknowledge the challenges and risks associated with Bitcoin adoption. Regulatory uncertainty, cybersecurity threats, and the potential for misuse in illegal activities are significant concerns that need to be addressed. Governments and regulatory bodies must work towards creating a balanced framework that promotes innovation while ensuring the protection of users and the integrity of the financial system.

In summary, Bitcoin holds significant promise for advancing financial inclusion, particularly in underserved and unbanked regions. Its decentralized nature, ability to facilitate peer-to-peer transactions, and potential as a store of value make it a valuable tool for promoting economic participation and financial stability. By addressing the associated challenges and fostering an environment of education and innovation, Bitcoin can play a pivotal role in creating a more inclusive global financial system.

Best Practices for Trading and Investing

Long-term vs. Short-term Strategies

The evolution of Bitcoin as a financial asset has been marked by significant price volatility, which has often been influenced by both long-term and short-term strategies employed by traders and investors. Understanding these strategies is essential for navigating the complexities of the Bitcoin market effectively.

Long-term strategies, often referred to as "HODLing" within the cryptocurrency community, involve holding onto Bitcoin for extended periods regardless of short-term price fluctuations. This approach is based on the belief that Bitcoin will appreciate significantly over time due to its limited supply and increasing adoption. Long-term investors are typically less concerned with daily or weekly price movements and more focused on the overall trend. They are driven by the underlying technology of Bitcoin, its potential as a global currency, and its role as a store of value. The primary advantage of this strategy is the reduction of transaction costs and tax liabilities associated with frequent trading. Additionally, it aligns with the original ethos of Bitcoin as a decentralized financial system that empowers individuals over institutions.

In contrast, short-term strategies involve frequent buying and selling of Bitcoin to capitalize on its volatility. Traders employing these strategies, often known as day traders or swing traders, rely heavily on technical analysis and market sentiment to make informed decisions. They use various tools and indicators to predict price movements and identify entry and exit points. The goal is to profit from short-term price swings, which can be substantial in the Bitcoin market due to its high volatility. While short-term trading can be profitable, it requires a deep understanding of market dynamics, the ability to react quickly to market changes, and a tolerance for risk. It also involves higher transaction costs and tax implications, which can eat into profits if not managed properly.

Both strategies have their merits and can be effective depending on the investor's goals, risk tolerance, and market outlook. Long-term strategies are generally suited for those who believe in the fundamental value of Bitcoin and its potential for significant future appreciation. These investors are less concerned with market timing and more focused on accumulating Bitcoin over time. They are often more patient and willing to withstand periods of volatility, trusting that the long-term trajectory of Bitcoin will be upward.

Short-term strategies, on the other hand, are better suited for those who thrive in fast-paced trading environments and are adept at technical analysis. These traders seek to exploit market inefficiencies and capitalize on short-term price movements. They must stay constantly informed about market conditions, news, and events that could impact Bitcoin's price. Successful short-term traders are often those who can remain disciplined, manage their emotions, and stick to their trading plans even during periods of high volatility.

Ultimately, the choice between long-term and short-term strategies depends on individual preferences and circumstances. Some investors may even combine both approaches, holding a core long-term position while engaging in short-term trades to take advantage of market opportunities. This hybrid strategy can provide the stability of long-term investing with the potential for additional gains from short-term trades.

In the context of Bitcoin, staying informed is crucial regardless of the chosen strategy. The market is influenced by a wide range of factors, including technological developments, regulatory changes, macroeconomic trends, and market sentiment. Investors and traders must continuously educate themselves and adapt their strategies to the evolving landscape. By doing so, they can make more informed decisions, manage risks effectively, and potentially enhance their returns in the dynamic world of Bitcoin trading and investing.

Leveraging Technology

In the evolving landscape of Bitcoin, one of the crucial aspects to understand is the intersection of regulation and decentralization. Bitcoin was created as a decentralized digital currency, promising freedom from traditional financial systems and centralized control. However, as its popularity and market capitalization have grown, so too has the interest of regulatory bodies around the world. This chapter delves into the emerging regulatory developments and their potential impacts on the Bitcoin market, aiming to provide a comprehensive understanding of the current regulatory environment and the future of Bitcoin regulation.

One of the most significant regulatory developments in recent years has been the increasing involvement of major financial regulatory bodies in the cryptocurrency space. Institutions like the U.S. Securities and Exchange Commission (SEC), the Financial Conduct Authority (FCA) in the UK, and the European Securities and Markets Authority (ESMA) have begun to implement frameworks aimed at overseeing and regulating Bitcoin and other cryptocurrencies. These frameworks are designed to address concerns related to market integrity, consumer protection, and financial stability. By establishing clear guidelines and standards, regulators hope to mitigate the risks associated with the volatile and often opaque cryptocurrency markets.

The SEC, for instance, has been particularly active in classifying and regulating digital assets. It has made strides in distinguishing between securities and commodities, thereby determining which assets fall under its jurisdiction. This distinction is crucial because it influences the regulatory requirements and protections that apply to different types of digital assets. The SEC's approach has generally been to consider many initial coin offerings (ICOs) as securities, thus subjecting them to strict regulatory scrutiny.

In Europe, the ESMA has focused on integrating cryptocurrencies into existing financial regulations. The introduction of the Markets in Crypto-Assets (MiCA) regulation represents a significant step towards creating a harmonized regulatory framework for digital assets across the European Union. MiCA aims to provide legal certainty for crypto-assets that are not currently covered by existing financial services legislation, while ensuring a high level of consumer and investor protection. It also seeks to support innovation and fair competition in the cryptocurrency market.

Another notable development is the approach taken by Asian regulators. Countries like Japan and South Korea have implemented comprehensive regulatory frameworks that provide clear guidelines for cryptocurrency exchanges and other market participants. Japan, for example, was one of the first countries to recognize Bitcoin as legal tender and to establish a licensing regime for cryptocurrency exchanges. This proactive regulatory stance has helped foster a safer and more transparent trading environment in these regions.

The implications of these regulatory efforts are profound. On one hand, clear regulations can enhance market stability and protect investors from fraud and manipulation. They can also help integrate Bitcoin into the broader financial system, facilitating greater acceptance and use of cryptocurrencies in mainstream finance. On the other hand, stringent regulations may stifle innovation and impose significant compliance costs on market participants. The challenge for regulators is to strike a balance between fostering innovation and ensuring market integrity.

As we look to the future, the trajectory of Bitcoin regulation will likely be shaped by ongoing developments in technology, market dynamics, and geopolitical considerations. The rise of decentralized finance (DeFi) platforms, for instance, poses new regulatory challenges due to their inherently decentralized nature and the difficulty of identifying accountable entities. Similarly, the growing interest of institutional investors in Bitcoin and other cryptocurrencies will drive demand for more robust regulatory frameworks that can provide assurance and stability.

In conclusion, the regulatory landscape for Bitcoin is evolving rapidly, with major regulatory bodies around the world playing an increasingly active role in shaping the market. These efforts aim to address the inherent risks and challenges associated with cryptocurrencies while fostering a safer and more transparent trading environment. As regulations continue to develop, it will be crucial for market participants to stay informed and adapt to the changing landscape, ensuring they can navigate the complexities of the Bitcoin market effectively.

Continuous Learning and Adaptation

In the ever-evolving landscape of Bitcoin, the dichotomy between short-term and long-term investment strategies stands out as a crucial consideration for market participants. Understanding and effectively implementing these strategies can significantly influence the outcomes of one's trading and investment endeavors.

Short-term strategies in the Bitcoin market often involve frequent trading with the aim of capitalizing on short-lived price movements. This approach is typically characterized by high volatility and requires a deep understanding of market trends, technical analysis, and rapid decision-making. Short-term traders, or day traders, often rely on technical indicators such as moving averages, relative strength index (RSI), and Bollinger

Bands to inform their trades. The goal is to enter and exit positions within a short timeframe, which could range from minutes to days, to maximize profits from price fluctuations. However, this approach carries inherent risks, including the potential for significant losses if the market moves against the trader's position. The volatility that short-term traders seek to exploit can also lead to rapid, unexpected shifts in market conditions, necessitating a high level of vigilance and quick reaction times.

Conversely, long-term strategies involve holding Bitcoin over extended periods, often spanning months or years. This approach is predicated on the belief in Bitcoin's potential for long-term appreciation. Long-term investors typically focus less on short-term price movements and more on the fundamental strengths of Bitcoin, such as its fixed supply, growing adoption, and the underlying blockchain technology. They may also consider macroeconomic factors, regulatory developments, and technological advancements that could influence Bitcoin's long-term trajectory. By maintaining a long-term perspective, these investors aim to ride out short-term volatility and benefit from the overall upward trend in Bitcoin's value. This strategy often aligns with the principles of "HODLing," a term derived from a misspelling of "hold" that has become synonymous with long-term investment in the cryptocurrency community.

The choice between short-term and long-term strategies depends on various factors, including an individual's risk tolerance, investment goals, market knowledge, and time commitment. Short-term trading can offer quick profits but demands constant attention and carries higher risks. Long-term investing, while potentially less stressful, requires patience and a strong conviction in Bitcoin's future potential. Diversifying one's approach by incorporating elements of both strategies can also be a prudent way to balance risk and reward. For instance, an investor might allocate a portion of their portfolio to short-term trades while holding the majority in long-term investments.

Ultimately, whether one opts for short-term trading or long-term investing, continuous learning and adaptation are essential. The Bitcoin market is dynamic and influenced by a multitude of factors, from technological advancements and regulatory changes to macroeconomic trends and market sentiment. Staying informed about these developments and being willing to adjust strategies accordingly can help investors navigate the complexities of the market and achieve their financial objectives. By combining a well-researched approach with disciplined execution, traders and investors can enhance their chances of success in the volatile yet potentially rewarding world of Bitcoin.

Conclusion

Summarizing Key Insights

In the realm of Bitcoin, understanding its market dynamics and the forces that drive its volatility is essential for any investor or trader. One critical aspect of this comprehension is recognizing red flags that signal potential market manipulation or unfavorable conditions. Identifying these red flags can help investors avoid significant losses and make more informed decisions.

One of the most telling signs of potential market manipulation is unusual trading volume. Sudden spikes in volume without any corresponding news or market events often indicate that something abnormal is happening. This can be a result of coordinated efforts by large holders, or "whales," who aim to manipulate the price for their own gain. By artificially inflating the trading volume, these entities create a false sense of market activity, luring unsuspecting traders into making hasty decisions.

Whales, or individuals and entities holding large amounts of Bitcoin, play a significant role in the market. Their trading activities can drastically influence Bitcoin prices. For instance, when whales decide to sell large amounts of Bitcoin, it can lead to a significant drop in prices, inducing panic selling among smaller investors. Conversely, when they buy in large quantities, it can create a price surge, drawing in retail investors hoping to capitalize on the upward trend.

Another red flag is drastic price movements within a short period. While Bitcoin is known for its volatility, abrupt and significant price changes that lack a clear cause should be viewed with caution. These can often be attributed to pump-and-dump schemes, where the price is artificially pumped up by coordinated buying and then dumped by massive selling, leaving regular investors with substantial losses.

The presence of spoofing and wash trading also signals manipulation. Spoofing involves placing large orders with no intention of executing them, simply to create a false impression of demand or supply. Wash trading, on the other hand, involves the same entity buying and selling an asset to create misleading activity. Both practices distort the true market picture and can lead to erroneous trading decisions by retail investors.

Moreover, the use of social media and online forums to spread misinformation or hype around Bitcoin should raise alarm bells. Often, manipulators use these platforms to create buzz around certain assets, driving irrational market behavior. Monitoring the sentiment on these platforms and verifying the credibility of the sources can help investors avoid falling prey to such tactics.

Lastly, the lack of transparency from exchanges can also be a red flag. Exchanges that do not provide clear information about their operations, such as their security measures, fee structures, or trading mechanisms, should be approached with caution. Intransparent practices can hide manipulative behaviors or operational inefficiencies that could impact the integrity of the market.

In conclusion, while Bitcoin's market is inherently volatile, recognizing these red flags can help investors protect themselves from manipulative practices. Staying informed and vigilant about unusual trading volumes, drastic price movements, spoofing, wash trading, misinformation, and exchange transparency are crucial steps in navigating the complex world of Bitcoin trading. Understanding the significant influence of whales and being aware of their potential impact on the market further equips investors to make more informed decisions and safeguard their investments from the hidden forces at play.

The Path Forward for Bitcoin

Bitcoin, the pioneering cryptocurrency, has carved out a significant niche in the global financial landscape. Despite its revolutionary potential and promises of decentralization, transparency, and stability, Bitcoin's market behavior often reveals a stark contrast to these ideals. The paradox of Bitcoin's extreme volatility, manipulated by powerful market players known as "whales," underscores the challenges it faces in achieving its original vision.

Whales, who control substantial portions of the Bitcoin supply, wield considerable influence over the market. Their coordinated buying and selling activities can create artificial price highs and lows, distorting the natural supply and demand dynamics. This manipulation not only results in significant price swings but also undermines the foundational principles of Bitcoin as a decentralized financial system. The tools and strategies employed by these manipulators, such as wash trading and pump-and-dump schemes, exacerbate market volatility and erode trust in the cryptocurrency market.

Despite these challenges, Bitcoin's underlying technology and potential for innovation remain compelling. Layer 2 solutions, integrating with traditional finance, and emerging technologies are critical avenues for Bitcoin's evolution. These advancements aim to address scalability issues, enhance transaction speeds, and foster broader adoption.

Furthermore, Bitcoin's role in financial inclusion cannot be understated. In regions with limited access to traditional banking services, Bitcoin offers an alternative means of participating in the global economy. Its decentralized nature can empower individuals and communities, providing a level of financial autonomy previously unattainable.

The geopolitical implications of Bitcoin are also profound. As nations grapple with the rise of digital currencies, Bitcoin's position in the global financial system continues to evolve. Countries are exploring regulatory frameworks to harness the benefits of Bitcoin while mitigating risks associated with its volatility and potential for misuse.

Looking ahead, the path forward for Bitcoin involves balancing innovation with regulation. Effective regulatory models must be developed to protect investors, ensure market integrity, and foster a stable and transparent trading environment. Continuous learning and adaptation are crucial for traders and investors to navigate the complexities of the Bitcoin market. Staying informed about market trends, recognizing manipulative patterns, and leveraging technology are essential strategies for success.

In summary, Bitcoin's journey is marked by both opportunities and challenges. Its potential to revolutionize finance is tempered by the need for greater transparency, regulation, and stability. As Bitcoin continues to evolve, addressing these issues will be key to realizing its promise and securing its place in the future of global finance.

Final Thoughts on Market Integrity and Stability

Bitcoin's journey as a revolutionary financial asset has been tumultuous, marked by extreme volatility and widespread speculation. As we look toward the future, it is essential to address the critical issues that have plagued Bitcoin's market integrity and stability. This final installment will focus on the necessary steps to foster a more transparent, fair, and sustainable Bitcoin market.

One of the primary concerns is the influence of "whales"—large holders of Bitcoin who can manipulate the market due to their substantial holdings. These individuals or entities can cause significant price swings through coordinated buying and selling, creating artificial highs and lows to maximize their profits. To counteract this, it is crucial to implement regulatory measures that increase transparency and accountability. By monitoring large transactions and implementing strict reporting requirements, regulators can mitigate the impact of whale manipulation.

Additionally, the role of technical analysis in Bitcoin trading has often been misused to deceive traders. Manipulative tactics, such as wash trading and pump-and-dump schemes, create misleading market signals that exacerbate volatility. Educating traders about these deceptive practices and promoting ethical trading standards are vital steps in protecting investors. Platforms should enhance their surveillance mechanisms to detect and prevent such manipulative activities.

The media also plays a significant role in shaping market sentiment. The spread of misinformation can lead to irrational trading decisions, contributing to market instability. It is imperative to establish standards for accurate reporting on cryptocurrencies and hold media outlets accountable for spreading false or misleading information. Encouraging investors to rely on verified and credible sources can help mitigate the impact of misinformation.

Dark pools and off-exchange trading mechanisms present another challenge to market transparency. These private trading venues allow large transactions to occur without public scrutiny, enabling market manipulation. To ensure a level playing field, regulators should enforce transparency in these trading mechanisms, requiring the disclosure of significant trades that could impact market prices.

The global regulatory environment for Bitcoin is complex and varied, with different countries adopting diverse approaches. Harmonizing these regulations and fostering international cooperation can help create a more stable and secure Bitcoin market. Establishing a global regulatory framework that addresses the unique challenges of cryptocurrencies while respecting the principles of decentralization is essential.

Finally, the path forward for Bitcoin involves embracing innovations and technological advances that enhance its functionality and security. Layer 2 solutions, such as the Lightning Network, can improve transaction speed and scalability, making Bitcoin more viable for everyday use.

Integrating Bitcoin with traditional financial systems can also enhance its legitimacy and accessibility.

In summary, ensuring market integrity and stability in the Bitcoin ecosystem requires a multifaceted approach. By addressing the influence of whales, curbing manipulative trading practices, promoting accurate information dissemination, enhancing transparency in trading mechanisms, and fostering a cohesive regulatory environment, we can create a more secure and fair Bitcoin market. Embracing technological advancements will further solidify Bitcoin's role as a transformative financial asset. The future of Bitcoin hinges on our collective efforts to uphold these principles, ensuring that it fulfills its promise as a decentralized, transparent, and equitable financial system.

Manufactured by Amazon.ca
Acheson, AB